Lois Snell

IN HIS PRESENCE

IN HIS PRESENCE ...

Witnessing the Glory of God

Lois Snell

IN HIS PRESENCE ...Witnessing the Glory of God

ISBN-13: 978-0-9707846-0-5

ISBN-10: 0-9707846-0-0

Scriptural references are taken from the King James Version of the Bible.

Cover design: Marvin Huckaby

Edited by: Lorre Antoine

WITH GRATITUDE

All praises and honor go to God in whom I have my being. I thank Him for the life He predestined I should live and for those lives, He strategically placed, that touched my own.

I'm thankful for and grateful to my daughters, Twyla and Amber, for their love and support; for listening to excerpts, reading chapters and manuscripts and offering their invaluable critique. I'm more thankful that, without my coercion, they've answered God's call on their lives.

Indeed, I truly appreciate the commitment to excellence of artist Marvin Huckaby who designed and created the book cover from reading the manuscript. And, much thanks to Lorre Antoine for editing the manuscript.

For these and others, all praises go to God.

CONTENTS

DEDICATION

To Sisters,
Cousins as sisters,
Brothers,
And to every ear
That will hear,
To every eye
That will see
Above And Beyond
Natural ranges
and
Distances.

PREFACE

Mama said I was born with a veil over my face. For many years I wondered if it were lace, silk, satin, linen or cotton. I wondered who'd removed it and what they'd done with it. Since it was a part of me, I felt they should've saved it to share with me at a later date. Then, I decided to dismiss it. Surely, I couldn't have been born with a veil over my face as laces do not grow in the womb. But, the spoken word would not lie dormant within my soul. Years later, I would learn that the veil Mama spoke of was not woven by the hands of man. It was woven of the Spirit.

There've been many days I've regretted not having documented the times I knew I was in the presence of God. Neither the date nor the hour seemed important at the time. It was always yesterday, last night or today and I was certain I wouldn't forget. As time is forever with God, He did not require that I remember exact dates or hours. The events that happened when I was in His presence were all that mattered. Those events are so embedded within my soul, I can never forget them.

I've shared openly with family, with friends and people in general the times I was in His presence. My family has been very supportive. They've witnessed times that I saw images and heard voices they did not see or hear. Many people are skeptical as it's very difficult to trust the unknown. I understand that. Yet, there are certain others who, intentionally or unintentionally, have tried to throw snares at me to cast doubt in my spirit. Their sole purpose is to make me question the very vision with which God entrusted me. They've asked, "How do you know it was God?" Though this served as a source of irritation more often than not, it is a valid question. I'd felt the answer was inherent, ingrained in one's subconscious--when you're in His presence, you know it's Him. But, I've come to learn that Satan often mimics God in hopes of deceiving us. Crafty and wickedly cunning, Satan's powers of persuasion are fine tuned to the point that he can confuse all except God's very elite. Satan's referred to himself as an angel of light, a day star. How do you know it's God? Jesus answers this best when He said:

"Beloved, believe not every spirit,
but try the spirits
whether they are of God:
because many false prophets
are gone out into the world.
Hereby know ye the Spirit of God:
Every spirit that confesseth
that Jesus Christ
is come in the flesh is of God."
1 John 4:1-2.

I find it very ironic and troubling that demons, Satan and his imps recognize the Holy One, yet many professing Christians do not. The following pages are an accurate accounting of the times I was in His presence.

GOING TO CUT'N DORA'S

Chapter 1

There were no streetlights in my hometown. There were no streets, just graveled roads and roads of clay. We lived in the last house on the last road. Electric lines had not yet reached our Clear Creek Community, which was five miles from the nearest small town, Valliant. We lived in country excellence with large wheat fields to our right and rolling acres of green and pine to our left. Behind our home all sorts of living foliage flourished underneath God's watchful eye. The land was speckled with dogwood trees, redwoods, elms and various fruit trees including persimmon and pears. There was an abundance of pecan, black walnut and hickory trees as well. Wild grapes were ripe for the picking and black berry vines lined the roads. We lived on forty acres and had two mules.

I had an adventurous spirit and loved to go exploring in the woods. I found streams, strange and beautiful trees and even a beaver's den I was certain no one had seen except me. Though Daddy often hunted for game for our table in those same woods, he listened with interest as I told him of my discoveries. Mama would clear her throat and warn me to stay out of the woods as bobcats, coyotes and wolves were sometimes spotted in our area. Anytime a bobcat or wild animal was spotted, Daddy would get his rifle and find him. And, I would go exploring in the woods.

Daddy and Mama, affectionately known as Crook and Sis in our area, were not my natural parents. They were married nearly thirty years and raised ten children of which only four were theirs. It seemed they were prime targets for anyone either un-willing or unable to accept responsibility for their own children. Daddy and Mama never turned anyone away. My birth mother died when I was three years old and my sister, Charlene, was two. My father sent us away from our birth home in Arizona, leaving siblings, grandparents, uncles and aunts behind. Daddy Charles sent us to live with his sister and brother-in-law in Oklahoma. In doing so, he severed all ties between my mothers' family and us for many years. Hence, my aunt and uncle became Mama and Daddy. They treated us as their own. Our home was filled with laughter and love—and work. Even with many children running around, Mama's house was kept immaculate. The chores were distributed evenly; although, she usually helped with my turn to do the dishes because I was slow. Not lazy--slow--in movements, not in mind. Saturdays were always washdays.

We lived off the land, butchering one cow and one hog yearly. We made our own sausage and cracklings. Daddy would then salt and cure the extra meats hanging the various cuts from large hooks in the smoke house. He loved to fish and, on one trip, he'd catch enough to fill a number two galvanized steel tub. He'd bring home catfish, trout, bass and tasty perch. Also, Daddy brought home tubs of buffalo that were half as big as I was. Cultivating our own garden, our bounty overflowed with every green thing imaginable. We grew mustard, turnip and collard greens. Polk salad grew wildly in the fields. We had separate potato patches, both sweet and Irish. Mama would roast sweet potatoes and we'd eat them with butter. Not commercial butter. Butter we'd churned for hours from clabbers, the spoil of sour milk that had once been sweet from the cow we'd milked. It was creamy and sweet. Mama canned everything we grew in clear Ball or Mason jars. Watermelon and cantaloupe we grew upon the hill. We never knew we were poor.

There was a spring of dancing waters not very far from our home. The spring bubbled up sparkling clear, cool water even on the hottest of days. This nature's wonder was God's handiwork bubbling up from the deep of Earth to provide drink for His people. It supplied our whole community with fresh water and never ran dry. People living in small towns five to twenty-five country miles away would sometimes come to Clear Creek and ask if they might have a small bucket of water. These people had running tap water in their homes; but, nothing quenched one's thirst like the freshly drawn dancing waters. Daddy and Mama were generous with everything. They were more than generous with their hearts.

The evening sun had long gone down and I'd not been able to explore that day. I sat staring out the window; my reflection was all that was shown; but, my mind's eye saw sunlight streaming down clay hills. These were the hills we'd sometimes lick and rub the residue on our cheeks for rouge. I saw a colorful array of wild flowers in patches of green grass with bright sunflowers taller than myself.

"Mama, may I go over Cut'n Dora's?"

"Girl, are you crazy? You know it's night time."

"But, I'm tired of being in the house. I want to go somewhere. Please, can I go over Cut'n Dora's? Please?"

Now, Mama wasn't the one to argue with. We knew all too well to keep our mouths closed once she'd spoken. But, she was in a jovial mood, so I pressed forward. Finally, she and Daddy agreed to let me go. Cousin Dora lived more than half a mile away and she was at least ten years older than Mama. I was seven years old at the time and by right, Cousin Dora and I had nothing to discuss.

"Okay, Lois. You tell Dora that I just made a batch of Tea cakes and she's welcome to have some," Mama said smiling at me. She and Daddy didn't really think I'd go—not at night. I could read it in their eyes. Glad to have a legitimate reason to visit Cousin Dora so late, I smiled brightly. Mama patted me on the head and Daddy winked at me as I stepped outside the door. My sister and cousins just looked at me like I was crazy while mumbling that I knew I wasn't going anywhere. I was determined to show them just who was crazy. Humming a sweet song, I left.

The front gate made its familiar screeching sounds and I crossed the cattle guard with ease. Fresh black berries scented the night air and I remembered that snakes loved berries. I heard the swishing of water as I neared the small pond where we caught crayfish and chased tadpoles with sticks. A bullfrog was bellowing in the near distance and I wanted to chunk a rock at him. Not needing to waste any time, I allowed him to make his night calls over the mound of chirping crickets. Darkness enfolded me as the man in the moon had chosen to hide his face. The hooting of an owl warned small prey he was on the stake out. And, I continued walking my familiar path. I'd climbed the little hill and was nearly finished climbing the big hill. Never before had I realized how far Cousin Dora's house was. Nearly half way there, the fear I'd rejected was coming to taunt me now. I swallowed the lump in my throat and clutched the three or four small rocks in my hand with which I'd planned to throw at the bullfrog. Nearing the little bridge, I knew certain danger lurked underneath. I knew the boogieman was waiting for me there. The big, bad boogieman that snapped little girls heads off with just one bite and broke boys legs with his fingers. Even though I tipped as lightly as possible when stepping on the bridge, I was certain he could hear the wild pounding of my heart. The boogieman could see through the darkness. And, the darkness of Clear Creek was blacker than death.

I wanted to turn, to go back home. But, remembering the smug looks on Charlene and Shirley's faces kept me focused. I tried not to breathe as I took my second step on the bridge. Suddenly, just beyond the bridge, there appeared a flashing of lights. Strange bright lights I'd never before seen. They were predominately white with many little sparks of color bouncing eagerly through them--pink, purple, blue and green--iridescent, soft and beautiful. The lights were about two to three inches wide and six inches long with a gentle curve facing each other as though they were a set. Drawn to the beauty of the sparkly lights, I forgot about the boogieman and walked toward them. Hoping to catch them and hold them in my hands, my eyes were wide with wonder when they began to move. I stepped toward them again and they immediately moved forward, keeping a distance of four to five feet ahead of me. Every time I'd move, they'd move, keeping on the path of the road. I liked the beautiful sparkly lights and, trying my best to catch up with them, I began to skip. The lights began to skip, also. The lights skipped ahead of me leading me straight to Cousin Dora's house, then disappeared on her porch.

"Well, Lois, what in the world are you doing here in the middle of the night?" asked Cousin Dora in surprise. She didn't wait for me to answer. "Come on in and have a seat, baby. Let me get you a dish of ice cream."

I sat down as she went to the icebox. The ice cream was a refreshing treat. I finished my dish wishing there were another bite or two.

"Mama cooked a batch of tea cakes today and she says you're more than welcome to some."

"Well, your mama is always cooking something or another. But, she sho' can make some tea cakes."

We talked about a little of nothing for about forty-five minutes to an hour. I was beginning to get worried about going home. I knew I was going to be afraid because my new friends, the lights, may not come back to brighten the way. I also knew I should be leaving and the longer I sat, the harder it would become. But, I continued to sit in safety and try to think of something to say to Cousin Dora. It seemed as though time stood still. Dreading the very thought of walking home in the darkness, I searched my mind for anything of interest to share. There was a frantic knocking at the door. Cousin Dora answered it and Mama and Daddy rushed in. Relief flooded my body.

"Lois, if I wasn't so upset, I'd whoop you right now! That's okay though, when I get you, I'll pay you for old and new," Mama said while grabbing me into her arms. Daddy smiled proudly at me.

"You know, your Mama and I thought you were kidding," he said.

"I know."

"We've been looking all over for you. We searched the smoke house, the chicken coup, the barn and even the tops of trees." Daddy grinned in amazement and I felt proud. He'd rescued me from treetops many a time.

"Don't you ever pull another stunt like that," Mama warned. "You could've been killed by a wild animal. You could've fallen into the creek and drowned, dark as it is out there."

"There was light, Mama."

"The moon is covered with clouds so where did the light come from?" Mama asked not concealing the fact that she thought I was lying as I had no flashlight. She listened quietly as I told her about the beautiful sparkly lights. I told her how they led me straight to Cousin Dora's house even though I hadn't shared with them where I was going. Also, I told her how they'd disappeared on the porch.

Mama knew that since God had created everything, He was capable of anything. That is, anything that is good and right, anything worthy to be done. Calming a young girl's fear in the deep of night was a small thing as He regularly poured out his glorious blessings on all manner of man and beast. She knew that we all had guardian angels to protect us, often from ourselves. Mama was thoughtful for a moment or so before she spoke.

"Angel feet."

"Thy word is a lamp unto my feet,
and a light unto my path."
Psalm 119:105

In Search Of The Lamb

Chapter 2

My room was always the hub of activity in our home. Winter or summer, the whole family gathered there for lively chatter. One wall held the full-sized bed that I slept in. There were four green chairs forming a perfect "X" around the cast iron, wood-burning heater that sat left of center of the room. Another wall held a small cot, and yet another held Mama's sewing machine, a trunk, and a couple of small tables. Daddy's rifle and shotgun collection was proudly displayed on the wall above the tables. Behind the heater, against the wall, was our stash of wood for the fire. On the other side of the heater was a double paned glass window with flowered curtains that were never closed. That window holds many precious memories for me.

I was generally the last person to go to bed. Mama didn't fuss with me about it because she knew I didn't require a great deal of sleep. Many a summer night, I was awakened from slumber to find brightness at the open window. Always, when I looked outside the window, there stood a beautiful white lamb staring in at me. Its fleece was brilliantly white--whiter than snow--free of all the country grit and grim animals were accustomed to. It positively glowed. The lamb's eyes would hold mine. They were filled with love and I could tell it liked me. It looked so warm and wonderful. I enjoyed the many nights he came to visit me. I wanted to be his friend, as he was already mine, coming to visit me and all. The strangest thing was, when the lamb looked into my eyes, I felt he could tell what I was thinking. He was glad that I liked him.

I'd never seen a lamb like that in the picture books or in my schoolbooks. Each time He'd come to visit me, our meetings were consistent. His marvelous light would wake me up. He'd stare into my eyes and I could feel the love of his heart. It was as though his whole being just radiated love. He never attempted to enter our home. He just stood peaceably outside looking through the window pane. The next morning, I'd jump out of bed and run outside in search of the lamb. We didn't have lambs on our acreage. I hadn't seen them on anyone else's, nor heard talk of anyone else having them. So, I knew this lamb had come from far away. It was probably lost and needed me to help him find his way. Surely, that was why he'd come to visit me. Sometimes I wondered how he managed to get upon the porch, especially after Daddy had screened the porch in.

I searched everywhere for the lamb, but could not find him. I searched the field where the cows were grazing. We had brown cows, some had white faces; but, for the most part, they were brown. I'd never seen the black and white spotted cows that were on the milk cartons. We lived in the country, so we had country cows. Those black and white spotted ones, those were city cows, I knew. The lamb was not hiding amidst the cows so I searched among the goats in the Briley's pasture. The lamb was not there. I went traipsing through the wheat fields. The golden stalks of grain were taller than me but they crunched and rolled down like carpet underneath the pressure of my feet. The lamb was not trapped inside. I searched every watering hole nearby, every pond and creek. I even went to the spring of dancing waters. The lamb was not there. In search of the lamb, I prodded through the woods, underneath the pine trees and in the ditches of clay. I searched the pecan grove, the hickory hill, fruit tree orchids and underneath the great shade trees. Closer to home, I checked the chicken coup, behind the barn and smokehouse. I searched the gardens, the potato and watermelon patches. Even the pigs had not seen the lamb. I searched everywhere but could not find him and I was very sad.

Mama, always busy, stood ironing clothes in the living room as I walked inside. She didn't look up from her ironing, but she knew something was troubling me.

"What's the matter?" she asked.

"I can't find the lamb," I sulked.

"There are no lambs in this area."

"Mama, there is a lamb. He comes to see me at night, waking me up from sleep, but I can't find him in the daytime," I explained. Mama set the iron up and looked into my eyes. She never made me feel foolish when I shared of things others did not see.

"What does this lamb look like?"

"He's beautiful. He glows like he has a light bulb inside him. His eyes are warm and filled with love--like a human's eyes, but, much better. It's like there's nothing ugly behind them," I told her. Mama didn't say anything. She watched me closely and let me talk. "He wakes me up at night, staring at me through the window. I know he wants to be my friend. But, when I go to find him the next morning so we can play, he's not there."

Mama rubbed my furrowed brows trying to soothe away the creases that had formed in my forehead. She knew I w a s telling the truth about the lamb. Oft times, children are too innocent to lie. They have no defense mechanism built in to define the unexplainable. Also, Mama knew it because she could read it in my troubled eyes. She pulled me closer to her. My arms went around her waist. She felt warm and comforting. She rubbed my thick plaits back and said, "Baby, that's just your mother checking up on you."

Many years later, I would come to learn that the glorious visitations of the lamb were not that of my natural mother. As beautiful and loving as she was, being human, she had no power over death. It had been Jesus, the Lamb of God, who'd flooded my soul with love and heightened my interest in seeking Him, in following Him. It had been Jesus who'd watched over me as I'd slept and kept even the hint of danger far from me.

"My sheep hear my voice,
and I know them,
and they follow me."
John 10:27

Mama And Daddy's Death

Chapter 3

Since there were no jobs or colleges readily available nearby my hometown, people would migrate to various parts of the world once they graduated high school. Mama and Daddy raised ten children. Only four were their natural children. Charlene, Shirley, and I (the middle group) were one-year stair steps with me being the eldest. At the appointed times, we'd moved to Oklahoma City, living for a time with my cousin and her husband. Bernice inherited much of Mama's gift of giving as from that day to this, her heart was open to people. In the deep of winter, she once gave the coat off her back to a total stranger who was waiting at a bus stop. We found jobs and moved out on our own once we'd saved enough money. Charlene and I shared a nice apartment. Shirley, Mama and Daddy's youngest natural child, also had a nice apartment approximately fifteen miles away. Having been raised in the same household, the nine of us were very close, more like sisters. John L. rounded us up to number ten and was the only boy raised in the family. Shirley came to spend the night with us as we'd planned to attend the same church service the following morning. For some reason, I was unable to attend and was home alone when the telephone rang.

I remember thinking that it must've been Charlene or Shirley calling to make sure my mind hadn't changed about attending church. In our rearing, it was not an option to stay home on Sunday mornings. At ten forty-five, they'd be extremely late if they were considering coming back to pick me up.

"Hello," I answered. "Lois?"

"Yes."

"Baby, this is Zader. Yo' Mama and Daddy is dead," spoke my natural father's wife. They'd moved to my hometown when I was fifteen years old and lived in Mama and Daddy's rent house just up the road from us.

"W-what?" I whispered, the breath gone out of me. I could hear her talking but couldn't distinguish the words. It was as though my word processing system shut down and I was only able to grasp bits and pieces. I did understand two words, shot and dead. I sat in shock, glaring at the telephone as though it were an evil beast, as though it had personally assaulted me. "Both of them?"

When she answered yes, I lost all control. A cry of anguish, foreign even to my own ears, tore from deeply within my being. The telephone fell from my hand and my body went on a destructive rampage. I attacked the dining room table with both fists, not feeling even the slightest stab of pain. I kicked the apartment walls and punched them with my fists. Like the police on a drug bust, I rammed the door with the full force of my body and shoulder. Running wildly throughout the apartment, I visited every room screaming with madness never before known and the depth of which could've never been imagined. As though aided by a trampoline, I jumped up and down continuously. Drowning in a sea of pain, I lost touch with reality. Nothing seemed real except the scorching tear of what seemed to be my soul. The beds needed to be kicked, tables needed to be turned over, toiletries needed to be knocked off the dresser. Or, so I felt. I ran from room to room destroying everything in my sight. My screams were constant in my ears. I jumped feet first onto my bed, then down to my knees. I bent over and started beating the mattress with both arms and fists. Perhaps, I was trying to kill death itself. Like a thief in the night it had come, robbing me of my most prized possession--the love and very lives of both my parents. Tears rolled like rivers down my cheeks and strange sounds continued to pour from within my throat. I was beating the bed with every ounce of force I could muster.

Out of the corner of my eye, I saw someone standing near the closet in my room. Unable to quit my vicious assault of the bed, I wondered how she'd managed to get into my home since the door was locked. I was relatively certain I hadn't let her in. She called my name and I just wanted her to go away.

"Lois," she called.

I tried to block out the sound. Who did she think she was anyway? Had I invited her in? What right had she to try to distract me from my destructiveness?

"Lois," she called again.

I didn't think I could've become more aggravated but she was making me mad. Not angry—mad! Didn't she see that I was busy beating the stuffing out of my bed? I had a job to do. I didn't have time to talk to her, didn't want to talk to her.

"You're going to hurt yourself," she warned.

Why didn't she just leave? Why didn't she just leave me alone in my misery, I wondered. Did I look neighborly--like I was eager to entertain? But, I didn't have the strength to acknowledge her or to scold her for intruding. I'd file an unlawful entry report with the police later. That would teach her to never again intrude on another's misery. It deeply offended me that she was there, secretly witnessing my pain, but I couldn't deal with her at this point. All I could do was cry and moan and beat my bed.

"Calm down, calm down. You're going to hurt yourself," she said. Her voice was soft and gentle. She possessed the calmness she was offering me. But, I was lost—lost in a place I'd never been. Lost in a place I'd never want to go. Trapped in pain, caged by misery. Lost.

"Mama wouldn't want you acting like this. She loves you, she wouldn't want you to hurt yourself," she said and I knew this was true. "Calm down, calm down. Do it for Mama and Daddy. Calm down."

My tears started coming in jerking sobs as I tried to gain some sort of control over my actions. She kept talking to me in soothing tones. Her voice, though calm, was filled with encouragement for the future. It was as though she was reminding me I had one, that mine wasn't lost with the death of my parents.

I was becoming more curious about her now. I was extremely curious about how she'd managed to gain entrance into my home--like a slithering snake. What really ticked me off was how she had the nerves to call my parents "Mama" and "Daddy." My fists began slowing down. I turned to look at her and was frozen for a moment--because SHE--was me. Me! Another Lois. She stood calmly against the wall talking to me while wearing my burnt orange pantsuit that had previously been hanging in my closet. She, the other Lois, wore her hair parted on the left and hanging neatly about her shoulders as did I. Her eyes--her face, she was me--the exact mirror image. I stared at her in total amazement, my violent actions subsiding. She could tell that she'd reached me. I read it in her eyes. Then, she was gone. I blinked in wonderment. How could this be? How could she have vanished before my very eyes? Where did she go, how did she go? She was just here!

A strange quieted calm came over me. Sitting down on my bed, I looked at the clock. It was eleven twenty. I went to my closet and opened it slowly, half expecting the other Lois to be hiding there, which she was not. My burnt orange pantsuit was still hanging neatly on the closet rod where it belonged. I double-checked the entry door and all the windows and they were securely locked.

It was then I remembered my step-mother was on the telephone. Understandably so, she'd hung up by the time I'd retrieved it. I returned her call and she shared with me what few details she knew. Daddy Crook was murdered in his bed as he slept. Mama Elma was murdered two bedrooms away beside the telephone. They'd been murdered with one of Daddy's shotguns. Mama was dressed for Sunday school, her purse and Sunday school book sat waiting on the bed like normal. She'd just finished preparing breakfast, homemade biscuits, sausage and eggs. Mr. Tedda, Daddy's best friend who lived up from us in the Briley's pasture, had found them. As he'd done for years, he'd come to walk with Mama to Sunday school. When we were young, he'd walked with us. Daddy didn't go to church often, but rather than hindering our spiritual growth, he encouraged it.

I felt numb and void of life. I tried to call my family but everyone was attending church services. At minimum, it would be two and a half hours before I'd be able to reach them. At least, that gave me time to set the house back in order.

"And the peace of God,
which passeth all understanding,
shall keep your hearts and minds
through Christ Jesus."
Philippians 4:7

Lois Snell

The Chiming Clock

Chapter 4

With the entirety of our relatives home for Mama and Daddy's funeral, sleeping arrangements were hectic. We were already a large family, but husbands and children had been added. One of my younger cousins, Charlene, Shirley and I were sleeping in the back bedroom where Mama was murdered. As usual, I was the last to go to bed. From the foot of the bed, I pulled the drawstring to the light and crawled up snuggling underneath the covers. The room was suddenly pitch black as there still were no streetlights or streets outside our home. We'd received electricity in our homes while I was in middle school. Tasting both sweetness and sadness of the familiarity of home, I turned to make myself comfortable. The antique dresser that had graced Charlene and Shirley's room ever since I could remember held the lovely old ivory clock. It sported lime green numerals and hands that illuminated from dusk to dawn. I remembered the beautiful chimes it once sang. It had awakened us every morning for school until I'd reached the tenth grade. At that point, it failed to run, to tick or chime and was retired to its rightful place on the antique dresser. It hadn't worked in almost seven years and I was surprised Mama hadn't thrown it out. Surely, she held on to it for sentimental reasons. After all, it was a gift her brother, my father, sent her. Finally, I drifted off to sleep.

In the midst of my sleep, I stirred at the familiar sounds of the chiming clock--thinking I was dreaming. At the correct increment of time, the chime rang out again. I knew I was dreaming then and allowed fantasy to count the five chimes while timing the seconds before the sound became constant, almost a shrill. I could no longer deny it. This was not a dream, nor was it fantasy, the clock working. Not only was it working, it was working in its old strength. I turned to sneak a peek at it but the clock was no longer on the dresser. The sound was coming from the bathroom; its door was near my head. The bathroom door was always closed and latched with a little iron hook when not in use. It had been closed and hooked when I'd gone to bed. Now, the chiming clock was in the bathroom while the bathroom door was ajar with a soft green light illuminating from it. At that moment, I was more frightened than I'd ever been in my life.

The tragedy of Mama's death, just days ago, in this very room was more than I could bear. Trembling and afraid, I eased the covers over my head and squeezed my eyes closed as tightly as I could. With the sound of the chiming clock still ringing in my ears, I nudged Charlene. I pinched her, punched and kicked her but she would not wake up. The sound was evidently exclusive to my ears. Neither my sister nor my cousins in the other bed awoke from the loud piercing shrills. And, I continued to try to hide from the sounds, from the green light, from fear itself.

I was paralyzed with fear while at the same time ashamed of myself for feeling it. The call of the unfamiliar had beckoned me since youth: It had protected me since youth. Yet, this was different, never before had the call been connected with fear. I called out to God for mercy. Sleep came.

Ringing early the following morning, the telephone awoke us. My cousin came in from the other room to answer it. Calling out to John L. and giving the phone to him, she immediately headed for the bathroom. The four of us sit up in our beds watching as he tried to get off the line. John L. replaced the receiver and walked from the room without acknowledging any of us. Just then, my cousin emerged from the bathroom with a huge smile on her face. Her eyes were aglow as she held the ivory clock up for us to see.

"Look, the clock is working," she exclaimed. Everyone was shocked and amazed that the chiming clock had been revived. I shared with them how the clock had been on the dresser when I'd gone to bed and how it had awakened me from a different location. Neither heard the chimes nor moved the clock.

For the remainder of our time down home, we'd periodically check on the ivory clock to see if it was still running. And, it was.

There is a four-hour drive between Clear Creek and Oklahoma City. Upon our arrival, I called my natural father to advise him that we'd made it home safely. After exchanging pleasantries, I asked if the clock was still working. The answer was no. The chiming clock had failed to run, to tick or even chime within thirty minutes of our departure.

NOTE: God's comfort and help comes
in many various forms. Often times
at the height of pain and fear,
it comes in the form of sleep.

"Thou art my hiding place;
Thou shalt preserve me from trouble;
Thou shalt compass me about
with songs and deliverance."
Psalm 32:7

Lois Snell

The Birth Of Twyla

Chapter 5

Long ago, the voice of wisdom stated that a woman was in her glory during her pregnancy. Her skin softens and glows: Her hair and nails grow at a faster rate. She becomes more focused on the importance of life and naturally craves what's best for her unborn child. And, God allows her whole body to blossom like the sweetness of a rose. All these factors were at play when I was pregnant with my daughter. In addition, I was physically fit. Beforehand, my girlfriends, Nikki, Joan and I played tennis on a regular basis. I rode motorcycles, hiked around the lake for the fun of it and chose walking to the grocery store for small purchases rather than driving. In addition, I jogged up the six flights of stairs at work instead of taking the elevator.

Unmarried and determined, I had no fear of raising my child alone. I knew the infant growing inside my womb would be happy and well-adjusted as I had more than enough love to share for two people. I welcomed my pregnancy as I'd welcomed life--with open arms. God had not given me a spirit of fear. (See II Timothy 1:7.) Therefore, fear and I had never been friends. I knew all too well how to toss it aside: I knew the importance of calling out to God when fear wanted to visit me. Yet, baggage of old played in the corners of my mind like a scratched and broken record that would not be ignored.

A few years after Charlene and I were born, my mother died in childbirth. The child, a son, also died. There were complications with Mom's pregnancy I was never aware of as a child and I'd grown up feeling the stigma that childbirth was to be feared. It brought certain death. It had claimed the life of my beautiful mother and I loved my mother--even now.

Throughout my pregnancy, I prayed for deliverance from this fear. It was foreign to me and I was totally uncomfortable with it. It was not that I feared death itself. I feared death leaving my child at the mercy of others. Everett and Elma Walker, near angels in the flesh, were now living in heavenly quarters. Although many carried brilliantly lit torches, I knew not one to stand in the gap that could outshine Daddy and Mama's candle.

I often wondered if God got tired of my asking for the same thing. I wondered if it were fair to ask. Never one to deny responsibility, I knew that hard labor was a prerequisite to childbirth. Yet, the fact that my mother died in childbirth was never far from my mind and memory out-weighed reason. I prayed that my child's father, who'd denied paternity, would bear the pain. For months, I prayed for a healthy, happy and beautiful baby. And, for months, I prayed her father would bear the pain.

As time drew near, my prayers increased. I made certain that everything was in order--just in case. One night I was mopping the kitchen floor and felt a few pricks of pain in my lower abdomen. It was just three or four little pricks that felt like someone sticking me with a dull stickpin. More water was on the floor. I was certain I'd mopped that spot. I mopped it again and still, there were a few drops where I was standing. I never felt the sensation of water rolling down my body but a bathroom trip confirmed that my water was trying to break. Finishing my chores, I showered and went to bed knowing the pains would wake me when it was time.

Evidently the excitement was too strong for sleep. I waited and waited, counting the little pricks and timing how often they were coming. And--I waited. The pricks were not getting stronger, just closer. I called my doctor and discussed my condition with him. He advised me to check into the hospital. Charlene drove me there and waited with me for a while. I insisted she go home, as she needed to go to work the following morning. Finally, she agreed to do so. I drifted off to sleep and was awakened from time to time by nurses doing their routine checks. I questioned the nurse about my lack of pain.

"Just wait until the water breaks," she informed me.

I was alone in my room--waiting. Waiting for something wonderful to happen. Waiting to become the mother I'd longed to be. Waiting to see the face that would capture my heart forever. Waiting to meet the little person that had so distorted my body. Waiting--for the pain. As I waited, the cries of others traveled through the hallways darting into every room where there were ears to hear. Their cries were whimpers, gut-wrenching screams, tear-jerking sobs, constant torturous moans and even blasphemous curses. I knew my time would not be long. As I waited, I prayed for the other mothers-in-waiting. I prayed to God to release their pain, to allow them to have a safe and fruitful delivery. I prayed that He would bless the mother and bless the child and fill their souls with His joy. My water broke.

The nurses were quick to check the vital signs, dilation status and record their findings. They told me not to be afraid and, at that moment, I realized that I wasn't. I prepared for hard labor by clutching the railing. And, as I clutched, the cries of others flooded my spirit. I looked to the ceiling, knowing the heavens were beyond, offering silent prayers for those women whose bodies were racked with pain. And still, I waited.

Before long, I was being transported to the delivery room. I saw the lights go flashing by--zoom, zoom, zoom--and knew the doctors were making a dreadful mistake.

"No, no, no! It's not time! I'm not hurting like I'm supposed to be hurting!" I cried in great distress.

They paid no attention to my outbursts but stayed to their course. They had their readings--they had their charts. They explained the procedure I'd signed for beforehand. They told me what to do, how to lie, when to push. I had no choice but to comply. I'd already been given the epidural. Prolonging the matter would distress my child. My mind was ablaze with concern for her safety. I continued to tell the doctors that I was not hurting like I was supposed to be hurting but my concerns fell on deaf ears.

Silently, I cried, "God, help me. Please help. They're going to do something wrong. I'm not hurting like I'm supposed to be hurting."

"It's a girl!" the doctor proclaimed at that very moment.

He placed a healthy baby onto my stomach as I strained to try to see. Tears of gratitude and praise rolled from my eyes.

"In my distress
I cried unto the Lord,
and He heard me."
Psalm 120:1

GOD'S ALARM

Chapter 6

When Charlene married Ray, he asked me to move in with them. They'd recently purchased a fabulous tri-level home in a prime location. The house was massive and beautiful. Since Ray worked the night shift, he knew Charlene would be afraid in the home by herself. After thoughtful consideration, I agreed to do so. Twyla and I stayed with them for approximately two years.

During that time frame, one certain morning blazes in my memory. It was during the wee hours of the morning and everyone had been asleep for hours. I was startled out of my sleep by a strange, undetectable noise. Immediately, I sprang out of bed and ran into the kitchen where the sound was loudest. Charlene arrived there approximately the same time. The room was filled with smoke. She ran back into her bedroom and woke Ray up. After quick advisement of the kitchen status, he came rushing in just as the blazes had taken off and were reaching for the cabinets. The brick wall behind the cook unit was already charred from heat. Seconds mattered before the whole room would've been engulfed with deadly flames. Ray worked quickly and knowledgeably to subdue the flames, thereby reducing damage and possible personal injury.

After much effort, the fire was extinguished, the hot spots cooled with water and the damage assessed. The three of us stood around talking, trying to pinpoint the cause.

“Well Ray, it's a good thing you installed that smoke detector," I said.

"We don't have a smoke detector," he replied. Charlene and I looked at each other in surprise. From different parts of the huge home, we’d both heard the alarm--loudly.

"Are you sure?" asked Charlene.

"I've been intending to buy some. I just hadn't gotten around to it," Ray advised her. We told him of the alarm we'd heard and he, too, stood in awe. Without doubt, we knew this had been God's alarm to keep us from harm.

"I laid me down and slept;
I awaked;
for the Lord sustained me."
Psalm 3:5

Lois Snell

TREAD MARKS

Chapter 7

Approximately one year after we'd moved into our own place, Charlene, Twyla, and I pulled into her circular driveway following a good day of shopping. I'd asked to borrow a pair of scissors and left the motor running while she'd run inside to get them. Since my sister was coming right back, she'd left the car door ajar.

Twyla hopped into the front seat when she saw the puppy coming toward the car. She leaned over to pet him and began to fall. Frantically, I reached for her only able to grasp a tiny bit of her garment. She slipped from my grasp and fell onto the hard concrete. When I'd reached for her, my foot accidentally came off the brake and the car rolled forward. My heart sank to unbelievable levels as I felt the back wheel roll over her tiny, three year old body. Those seconds it took me to put the car in park and run around to her seemed like an eternity. I just knew my child was crushed, possibly dead--at my hands.

Twyla was lying on the concrete whimpering--not crying aloud. I feared she was too hurt to cry out. Charlene ran outside and was alarmed by the sight. It was obvious what had happened. She became frantic as I looked Twyla over and picked her up. Playing in the back of my mind was wonder if I should move her or wait for the trained hands of the paramedics to arrive. That would take too long, I knew. From the time of the accident to the time she was in my arms took less than one minute, less than sixty slow seconds. I rushed her to the emergency room at the nearest hospital.

The emergency ward was slow that night for which I was grateful as there were no delays in seeing my daughter. Even then, God was protecting us. The doctors asked countless questions and did all the necessary tests and X-rays. They told me it was impossible that I had run over her. I wanted them to be thorough with her exam. I couldn't bear the thought of waking up in two hours and finding my daughter dead. I explained over and over again that the tire had actually rolled over her, that I felt the lump.

"Ms. Snell, there are no broken bones, neither fractures nor splinters. There is not even discoloration of the skin nor swelling or heat to the touch. If your car had rolled over her, there would be some signs," the doctor said in tones that clearly showed his annoyance with me.

I grabbed her clothing and thrust them in his face. Twyla had worn an apricot one piece pants jumper, white socks and little sandals. The apricot jumper clearly showed the dark tread marks of the tire. Also, her sandals showed scrapings that had not been there previously. The doctor stood looking at the tread marks on Twyla's clothing in disbelief. All his medical expertise and scientific wording escaped him. Without further insistence from me, he re-examined her--more thoroughly than before. His findings were the same. There was no physical evidence that she'd been run over by a car.

He told me to take her home, to wake her every two hours and make sure she was coherent. Also, he advised me that she should be able to move her limbs freely. If she experienced any abnormal discomfort, swelling or vomiting, I was to call him. And, he gave me his personal number.

I let Twyla sleep in my bed that night, waking her every two hours, praying in between. Still fearing the worst, I didn't go in to work for the next few days. It was not an option to leave my precious daughter in the skilled hands of the Christ-centered daycare employees I'd thus far trusted. Some situations only warrant a mother's touch and this was one of them. Twyla turned out to be fine though she developed fluid on her knee from the accident. Her doctor said it should dissipate without aid. After approximately three weeks had passed and it had not, I took her in to have the fluid drawn out. Twyla was a true champ about the whole incident. To keep the swelling from returning, she had to wear an ace bandage wrapped securely around her knee and leg for a while.

Twyla became the recipient of many sympathetic words from strangers as well as those we knew. Having always been taught to tell the truth, she was straight forward and to the point. Sometimes the truth is brutally disturbing. Often, strangers would ask her what happened to her leg.

"My Mama ran over me," was always her answer. When they gave me disapproving and sometimes downright dirty looks, I didn't bother to defend myself. What would be the point?

During this accident and shortly thereafter, I did not see miracles descending from the sky. I did not see angels bridging their hands between my daughter's clothing and her small body to keep it from harm as the tire rolled over her. I did not see the Holy One lay hands on her and restore the damage that had been done by the weight of the car. I saw the tread marks on her clothing. I saw her body, whole and free. I knew we'd been in the presence of God.

"He shall cover thee
with his feathers, and
under his wings shalt thou trust:
his truth shall be
thy shield and buckler."
Psalm 91:4

Lois Snell

The Fall Of Destruction

Chapter 8

Quickly I found out how difficult it was to support a child on a single income. Before my daughter was born, I'd sometimes worked two jobs to make major purchases. Now, I found it necessary to hold a second job just to pay daycare. Formula and diapers were far more expensive than I'd imagined and it was important to me that my child had beautiful clothing. She was a beautiful child and deserved only the best. Though she was fatherless, I was determined she would not feel fatherless. Much later in life, I learned that two jobs didn't alleviate the reality, financial or otherwise, of being fatherless. It contributed to the feeling of being also motherless.

My whole way of life changed. I'd been taking college classes at night and gave those up to work extra hours. I began to frequent garage sales, purchasing items that I was either too cheap or too poor to pay full price for. Poor only in terms of finances, I was wealthy in things that really mattered--love and spirit. I'd always had an eye for beauty. At garage sales, I purchased antiquities, seasoned heavy pots and pans, and decorative items. I blended the old with the new and the outcome was warm, inviting and beautiful. It's called eclectic now, that look which many designers are being sought to fill. There was always an on-going home project. I painted walls, hang wallpaper, laid kitchen tile and repaired damaged areas in drywall. I even installed my own ceiling fans. I'd never taken a course in home repair but God blessed every project I took on. I loved working in the house. I loved making it perfect for my daughter and me. God blessed me with untiring energy. We went to church on Sundays, but the spirit of God was daily alive in our hearts.

My family often scolded me for working two jobs. They couldn't perceive that I needed the extra income to make things run smoothly. They were all married by then, with children. One of my cousins stated that I was too close to my daughter. She said that I loved Twyla too much, claiming I was smothering her and putting her before God.

"When you put others before God, He'll take them from you," she said.

My aunt came for a visit from California. She'd been there for two hours and had not conferred with my other relatives, but she told me virtually the same thing. I did not believe this was the case but the thought frightened me. I didn't feel I was any different than any mother should be. Yes, I loved my daughter. Yes, I'd do everything in my power to make certain her life was a good one. I wanted her to have happy memories as I did. As far as smothering her, I did keep a close eye on her. That's what mothers are supposed to do. I looked at the situation long and hard. I took the matter to God in prayer and asked for forgiveness had I done wrong. He did not advise me to change my course. God knew He was alive and faring well in my heart. Furthermore, He'd chosen Twyla to become my daughter so she would be a recipient of all the love, protection and warmth I had to offer. Nothing is by chance.

Late one night, Twyla was asleep in my room. I was nearly finished decorating her room and was determined to finish that night. I was hemming a table cover for the round table that sat beside her brass bed. The room was beautiful. It held a beautiful antique dresser on one wall. Her huge toy box, rocking horse, and tea table set filled another wall. The purple shag carpeting complimented the soft pastel pink walls. Her bedspread and curtains were white based displaying a beautiful watercolor floral print, with emphasis on pink. I'd purchased an extra coordinating sheet to make the table cover. As time permitted, I'd worked on this room for the previous two weeks.

While working on the hem, something slammed to the floor just behind me with so much force it jarred the room. Startled, I turned to see what could've made such a heavy impact. There was nothing there. I looked to the ceiling but nothing had broken through. As I looked around the room, everything was intact. Curious, I went to the other side of the bed to see what had fallen. Again, there was nothing there. I knew I wasn't going crazy. I'd heard that crash as well as felt the tremendous jarring. Looking underneath the bed, nothing was to be found. I decided to rub my hand across the carpeting where the crash had landed. The carpeting was warm to the touch, as though a body had very recently lain there.

The following morning I called my cousin, whose house I was renting, and shared the details of the strange crash with her. I asked if similar incidents had happened when she'd lived there. Her answer was no, but she tried to make me understand it. She reiterated that I was too close to my daughter and said she felt God was trying to get my attention to warn me to change. I listened quietly and tried to learn from her rationale but it didn't set well within my spirit. I'd already taken this matter to God. Throughout my lifetime, He'd guided my steps through visions and dreams and I knew this was not an area in which He felt I was lacking.

The fall of destruction continued to trouble me for a time. Although I'm a highly spiritual person, I want conclusive answers to most questions. In order for me to be strong for my daughter, I needed to be strong within myself. I could not allow fear to creep into my spirit. It was not an option. God had not given me a spirit of fear. I'd use this Scripture whenever a frightening situation would occur. It served to stabilize my mind and kept me grounded in my faith. God had not given me a spirit of fear. From the printed words of the Bible and from life, I knew this.

As time passed, I realized what had happened that night. I've always known that I'm a child of the Most High God. God has always known that. Just as God and I have always known this fact, the evil one soon learned. Satan is not omnipresent as God is. He gained this knowledge from studying my actions and interactions with others. Satan wanted to destroy me that night. He'd deliberately sent a demon to invade my home with the sole intention of destroying me. Just as the demon positioned itself to strike his deadly blow, I believe God instructed his angel to cast him down from his evil intentions. The deadly blow I'm referring to could've shown up as a heart attack, stroke, aneurysm or any number of swift and fatal illnesses. Yet, God fought for me. He fought and won the battle I hadn't realized had been waged against me.

We deal with dangers both seen and unseen on a daily basis. The evil one is crafty and cunning and will quickly use unseen forces to defeat us. Never place limitations in your mind by believing only that which can be seen with the natural eye. You feel the effects of the wind as it blows against your face. You don't see it, yet you know it's there. So is the evil one, always there lurking in invisibility while plotting your demise. He is real.

***NOTE**:* God will always be bigger and
more powerful than your greatest foe.

"The Lord shall fight for you
and ye shall hold your peace."
Exodus 14:14

Spoken To About Amber

Chapter 9

It seemed that everyone was concerned about my marital status, or lack thereof. All my family and the majority of my friends were married. They continued to supply an endless list of resumes of male suitors that I promptly rejected. They didn't understand that I didn't need to be married to be happy as I'd never needed to define myself as Mrs. Somebody. I enjoyed making my own decisions and paying my own bills even though it often took two jobs to do so. It bothered my family and friends that I continued with both jobs. I suppose they felt a husband would replace the second job; yet, I knew that a husband, who wasn't the right one, would demolish the peace and joy I felt.

Year's prior, at age fifteen I'd been molested and raped by someone trusted by the family. For a time, I was too ashamed to speak out. Once I did, handling of the situation was not precisely in my favor as it protected the predator. The informed adults saw that I was no longer in that environment. But, they saw no reason to shame the family and disrupt lives by publicizing private matters. So, I knew firsthand the tinkering of a man's heart. I realized that all men were not self-serving, self-centered and evil, of course. Yet, my standard of measurement, Daddy Crook, was extremely high. In all my adult years, I'd not met one that compared in character, dedication, honesty and genuine warmth and love.

Though my lips remained silent for many years, the degradation I'd felt in my heart was ever afresh. Molestation and rape are not crimes that leave its victims unscarred. There's not always physical scarring easily seen with the naked eye as was true in my case. Yet, scarring does occur. It's prominent in emotions, in fears, in the inability to trust others. Emotional scars are often too deep to heal. This is especially true if counseling is not sought. We who've experienced it exist wearing the pretense of happiness while feeling like flawed roses inside. So, we mentally block out the memories and they return to torture us years into the future.

My daughter was quite young and I was not willing to put her at risk. I was not willing to fall asleep at night wondering if my husband, not her natural father, slept throughout the night. Wondering if, as I slept, he ventured into areas where he did not belong.

I had baggage. And, baggage can either destroy your tomorrows or become roadmaps of pitfalls to avoid. I chose the latter. It would take a very special, wonderful person to chisel away the ice I'd allowed to form around my heart. Even then, he would have to gain the trust of a seasoned untrusting heart.

My cousin's husband was determined that I should not spend my life alone. He had many single friends that were intelligent, good breadwinners, fun loving and optimistic. I advised him that I was not interested in his friends. He was very persistent and at every opportunity continued to highlight their wonderful attributes. After careful consideration of his handpicked choices, I agreed to meet Phillip. Contrary to several others, I'd not met Phillip before but was assured he was a good man. I'd decided on Phillip because I liked the sound of his name. Prior to our meeting, Phillip and I spoke for a few times by telephone and I liked the sound of his voice, also. We worked different shifts so neither of us was readily available on a whim. The night we met was between shifts. I'd invited him over for a drink--Coke or Pepsi. He was given a choice.

The first thing I see, and often the only thing I see, is a person's eyes. I read them. I was clueless as to what Phillip looked like. Since that did not define character, it'd never been a major concern of mine.

Yet, I was pleasantly surprised when I'd answered the door. The man was undeniably handsome. His eyes were warm, and I knew love resided within his being. I invited him in.

As I stepped aside, the telephone rang and I headed toward the kitchen to answer it. Upon my return, Phillip was leaning against the door as if he were posing for GQ Magazine. He wanted to give me a photo image of rugged but polished masculinity at its finest. His rich mahogany skin positively glowed. Phillip's high cheekbones and pronounced nose would've been magnificent lines for the sculptor's hands. Soft and full lips--they were sensual even to the eye. His black mustache and perfectly trimmed beard highly accented the richness of his skin. Phillip wore a brown and white African print short set that proudly exposed his hairy, muscular legs. The top few buttons of his shirt were left undone to emphasize the expanse of his hairy rich chocolate chest, of course. Eye candy. I snapped the visual image and quickly filed it away to be retrieved at a later date.

The grin of confidence was on his face. Suddenly, I was filled with revulsion. It was not that he wasn't appealing; he was greatly blessed in that area. But, the fact that he used sex appeal to attempt to lure me into his web appalled me. After all, this was a first date and I was not a quick lay. Never having liked wasting my time, I immediately knew this was going nowhere. I wondered if it were possible that I'd misread him. I was short with Phillip and ended the meeting sooner than planned.

He didn't call me for three days yet I was not concerned. Actually, I was still angry that he had the gall to show up wearing shorts. He was not the one. Then, the telephone rang.

"Hey, this is Phillip," he said, his voice low and sexy. "What's going on?"

"I'm busy."

"I'm told you don't do anything but work and go to church." He chuckled. "So, what are you so 'busy' doing over there?"

I tried to think of something smart to say. Never having been prone to lies, I couldn't. When I hadn't answered in a fair amount of time, he laughed softly.

"Did I offend you in some way?"

"Why did you come over here in shorts?" I exclaimed in anger. Phillip roared with laughter. Though still angry, the sound of his laughter began to soften the lines of my face.

"Did that bother you?"

"I thought it was very rude," I said.

"I have--other clothes," he said, laughter still mingling in his voice. We talked quite a while longer and set another date.

When he arrived this time, he was respectable. We went out for dinner and I enjoyed his company. When we returned, we talked at length about our lives. He talked about employment--past and present, sports, future plans. I was interested in family and took note that he'd avoided that topic. Already knowing he had three daughters, I asked what visitation arrangements he and his ex-wife made with the children. His eyes darkened and I could see there was pain hiding behind them. It was obvious that this was not a topic he chose to share. I watched him closely while waiting for an answer. Phillip advised me that he and his wife had been separated for two years and there were no plans for reconciliation.

My eyes widened as I sat back in my chair in total shock. I'd just gone out with a married man! I was twenty-eight years old and had just broken my first dating rule. He sensed how disturbed I was. Phillip took great pains to assure me that his marriage was over and they'd be getting a divorce soon. A week passed before I accepted his call. I needed time to think.

During that time, I'd spoken with my cousin's husband and he'd confirmed that Phillip and his wife had indeed been separated for two years. He and Phillip had known each other for many years. They were friends but he was my family. He would have nothing to gain by confirming Phillip's lies. I felt I could trust his judgment. But, even the best of friends never truly know what lies deep within the heart of another. He, too, was surprised as the events of our lives began to unfold. I'd never known or heard of anyone who'd been separated for two years. I couldn't imagine anyone willingly wasting that much time. Therefore, I reasoned the marriage must truly be over. So, I let down my shield and enjoyed my time with him.

We appeared to be a perfect match. We spent most of our free time together and I was happier than I'd ever been. My living room sofa was nine feet long. Phillip would sit at one end and I at the other and we'd talk for several hours at a time without running out of things to say and without touching. You just know it's real when intimacy is not involved and words, thoughts and ideas keep flowing. I found him to be interesting, intriguing, knowledgeable and warm. Laughter seemed to have my name attached to it when Phillip was over. We shared everything, including what I felt was our innermost thoughts. Twyla was beginning to see what it would be like to have a father around. He was good with her, loving and warm. Likewise, I was beginning to see what true family life would be like and loved the feeling. Phillip was my soul mate, and I fell deeply in love.

Months sped by in record time. After learning I was pregnant, I became angry with myself. Not with Phillip, not with my unborn child--only myself. I'd never been able to understand why people blamed others for their own actions. Phillip had a fifty percent vested interest in this, but I was only aware of my responsibility. He was not the least bit surprised to learn the news and had a knowing grin on his face when I'd emerged from the doctor's office.

Once we stepped outside, Phillip pulled me into his arms and gave me a long sensuous kiss. "You going to give me a son?" he teased.

I didn't answer. The reality of the moment was sinking in--fast. As he drove home, I was deep in thought. My pregnancy forced me to look at this situation logically. Phillip was still a married man. It had been some time since I'd heard him mention his divorce. I already had one child I was sole support of. How could I afford a second child? By experience, I'd learned I couldn't depend on men. What if--at the eleventh hour--Phillip decided it convenient to claim sterility, too?

The happiness and joy I'd felt for months disappeared quickly. This was a serious situation. Then, I began to hear rumors that Phillip was trying to reconcile with his wife. He denied it, of course. But our time together wasn't what it'd been. He'd stopped giving me checks to help pay bills and started giving me cash. So, I knew something was going on.

The thought of abortion entered my mind and was quickly kicked aside. My child wasn't at fault here, I was. The pressure of how

I'd be able to manage weighed heavily upon my heart. If Phillip and his wife did reconcile, where would that leave my child? Would he attempt to get joint custody? Unlikely. Full custody? Not an option. I knew I'd have to be sole support of this child as well and was gravely concerned about where she'd fit in his life. I wondered if he'd ignore her and pretend she was never born. I wondered if he'd shun her in lieu of his other children. I knew of cases where men did this dastardly thing. These thoughts levied heavy pressures upon my heart and mind. Suddenly, I began to notice all the abortion references on television, in magazines and newspapers. It was legal in our state. Legality and ethics are worlds apart.

I approached Phillip with the idea and he was appalled at me. He said, "Not with my child!"

Phillip promised that I wouldn't have to raise our child alone. He spoke brightly of our future together as a family. I desperately wanted to believe him; yet, I was almost certain he was taking no steps toward his divorce. The next few weeks were a ball of confusion. I honestly could see no way my finances could stretch to cover daycare for two children, plus all the essentials a new baby would need. Child support was an option, but Phillip already had three children. The support I'd be awarded would do little more than scratch the surface. I'd always been against people bringing children into adverse situations, whether deliberate or not and had never excluded myself from my own convictions. Still, at this point, I had not ceased to be angry with myself for becoming pregnant.

I'd been raised in a Christian home. I'd always been taught to take my cares to Christ in prayer. At this moment in my life, I was living in the belly of sin. I knew I was living in sin, loving it, and was not willing to cleanse myself of it. I wanted Phillip in my life. The thought of going to Jesus, the Christ, about the matter didn't enter my mind. I knew what His answer would've been had I cast my cares upon Him. That answer would've proven too high a cost to pay. So I didn't allow my mind to venture there. I tried to handle the situation myself. Rather than Jesus, I sought council of my friends.

One of my friends called, gave me the name, phone number and address of an abortion clinic in our area. She said, "I don't want to talk about it. You know you can't afford it. You know *HE'S MARRIED!* Don't you be caught holding the bag. Call the number!" She hung straight up in my face.

Looking like the picture of gloom, I carried the number around in my purse for a few days, taking it out and staring at it from time to time. Time was of the essence. I came to believe this was my only option and decided to go forward with it.

When Phillip called, I told him I'd decided to have the abortion. I knew what to expect because he'd talked me out of it three times already.

"H-m-m. All right," he said thoughtfully. "Let me know how much money you need."

I hung the telephone up in his face and burst into tears. What was wrong with him, I wondered. Surely, he must be crazy! He was supposed to talk me out of it--again. He was supposed to talk me out of it as many times as it took! That was his job. I was in such instant turmoil that my head ached. As I was crying, I heard a small weak voice say, "Mama, don't." And, I screamed out in agony, with uncontrollable wailings one would associate with death. Others may have called it their conscious, but, I knew this was the voice of my unborn child.

"Lois, why are your crying?" spoke the voice of God, rich with authority. Babbling like a drunken fool, I sat up in bed, rubbing my eyes; yet, the tears continued to flow.

"I don't know."

"Are you hurt?" God asked.

"No."

"Are you hurting?"

"No," I answered.

"Why are you crying?" God asked again.

I could barely talk. The deep hurt I was feeling made my body weak and I was trembling, knowing nothing is hidden from God. He knew why I was crying far better than I. He wanted me to admit it to Him. I managed to pull my legs up underneath my chin and wrap my arms around them and the bedspread. I was trying to stop my trembles and answer God in all truth.

"I—I just really don't want to—kill my baby."

"Then, *why* are you doing it?" God asked. My tears suddenly dried up, my trembles stopped and I could think clearly. Twyla was nearly four years old and we'd made it just fine. God had seen to it that we had. I reasoned that if I could make it with one child, I could make it with two. God did not speak another word at the time. He'd restored my thought pattern to that which was right and left me to make the right decision--the decision of life.

NOTE: If God blessed the seed,
He'll bless the life. God is pro-life.

"Now, I know that the Lord saveth his anointed;
He will hear him from his holy heaven
with the saving strength of his right hand."
Psalm 20:6

Lois Snell

The Birth Of Amber

Chapter 10

The breaking of the waters came as I spoke with my cousin on the phone. I'd complained of a few little cramps and she took notice that I'd made three bathroom trips during our conversation. She realized what was going on before I had.

"Girl, you're in labor," she said.

We continued our conversation, both timing the pains and bathroom trips. She was at work but said she'd be right over to take me to the hospital. Having picked up another cousin on the way, they attempted to keep me laughing to rid my mind of the pain. Both stayed at the hospital until Amber was born. They attempted to reach Phillip and other family members to advise them of the good news. Their lips continuously flowed with humorous tales. Sometimes my stomach ached from the pain of laughing too much.

God aided me with delivery of both my children. I experienced the normal pains associated with childbirth this time; yet, fortunately they only lasted four hours. Just four long, agonizing hours. Still, I remember how wonderful and competent the nurse was. The delivery staff was short on nurses that day. To make matters worse, it seemed as though this was the day of choice for every pregnant woman in the area. The delivery ward appeared more like an emergency ward as some ladies were forced to lie in the hallways since all delivery rooms were filled. Thankful to have arrived early enough to be placed in a room, I was aware of the others plight, but this time my prayers were for myself--for the unrelenting pain I was feeling.

I don't know if it was from fear, the heavy pains piercing through my body, or a combination of both, but the epidural didn't take and I told the doctors I could still feel the pain. They didn't truly believe me but they did a series of tests to see if I still had feeling in my lower body. When I answered positively to each touch and negatively to each non-touch, their eyes met in surprise. I was given another, and this one worked.

Amber looked like a miniature version of Twyla at birth. Fluffy black ringlets crowned her beautiful face. I was pleased and happy she was alive and breathing on her own. Her birth was a sweet and joyous occasion. My body went into almost immediate shock afterwards. I was shivering cold with chattering teeth. Yet, I still remember my cousin catching my hand and saying, 'She looks just like Twyla.' She voiced the first confirmation of my own thoughts.

When we were released from the hospital, Phillip stopped by his mother's and two of his sisters' homes to show off his new daughter. They held her closely and marveled at how lovely she was. Phillip was very proud of her, and I appreciated him more and more. The final stop before the destination of home was at the Christ-centered daycare where Twyla was. The workers rushed out to the car to get their first peek at Twyla's newborn sister. Twyla's eyes were filled with delight and love as she caught her first glimpse of Amber. At home, Phillip picked Twyla up and sat her in the middle of the bed. He then took bundled up Amber and placed her onto Twyla's lap, instructing Twyla how to hold her. Knowing Twyla, at four and a half years, was too young to hold a newborn, I was filled with concern.

"Twyla, this is your little sister, Amber," Phillip explained. My heart was overjoyed as he explained the importance of sisterhood and how important she, Twyla, was and would always be in the family. It hadn't dawned on me that siblings needed a formal introduction or that the older child may feel rejection since so much attention would be given to the younger. These thoughts hadn't entered my mind because I knew my love was full and pure for both my children. Others had mentioned that Twyla may be jealous when the baby was born but I didn't see that as an option.

Phillip moved in with us. He attended technical school during the day and worked at night. His schedule was busy, but he made sure he had quality time with Amber. He'd feed her, change her diapers, bathe her and rock her to sleep. I enjoyed watching them together. Sometimes when she cried, I'd pretend to be asleep so I could secretly watch him take care of her. Phillip spoiled both Twyla and Amber with loving and genuine fatherly affection. My love and appreciation for him continued to climb.

Twyla had a white poodle for a house pet, Pierre. During the final trimester of my pregnancy, Pierre had been banished to the backyard and garage. I didn't like the idea of a dog in the house with a baby. He was not thrilled about his new living quarters but had adjusted by the time Amber was born. Several times as I cared for my infant child, I'd see Pierre out of the comer of my eye--watching us. He'd stand quietly in a corner or near a chair and watch, never making a sound. As long as I was still, he was still. When I'd turn toward his direction, he'd be gone. Now, this was not our pet, this was an angel watching over us. Our pet had no way of obtaining entrance into the home and, he was always still outside when I'd peep out the window to check on him. I was not afraid of Pierre. Since I knew he was an angel, I decided to time his visits. The longest time was thirty minutes. I believe he would've stayed longer had I not needed to move. I'd fed Amber and rocked her to sleep. Pierre was standing in a corner approximately twelve feet away. For the first time in all of his many visits, I looked directly into his eyes and he was astonished. She can see me, I read in his eyes. Pierre vanished, right before my eyes. The angel never appeared in Pierre's form again.

"To everything there is a season,
and a time to every purpose
under the heaven:
A time to be born…"
Ecclesiastes 3: 1-2

Jesus, The Silent Passenger

Chapter 11

Seldom, if ever, does anything end up right when it starts out wrong. As the months rolled by, I thought Phillip and I were making great progress. Our home was filled with warmth, love, and tenderness. The lines of communication were never broken between us and there was nothing to argue about. He'd advised me that the divorce was in progress. I'd actually seen some of the documents and he'd openly discussed their day in court with me. I was patiently waiting for his divorce to be finalized so we could be married.

While doing the laundry some time later, I noticed there were only a few items belonging to Phillip that needed washing. Curious, I went to Phillip's closet and opened the door. At least half his clothing were missing. Realizing he was leaving me, I stood in shock for more than a few moments. Shock turned into anger.

"You don't have to sneak." I said to the closet. "I'll help you to go."

Finding a large box in the garage, I neatly packed all his belongings so he would not need to return for them later. Also, so they wouldn't clutter up my house. Most importantly, so there would be nothing of his I'd be able to stare at longingly.

As I waited for him to return, I called his mother. We had a good relationship; she treated me like a daughter. She also treated Twyla and Amber the same--cherished granddaughters. I'd never questioned her about certain aspects of Phillip's life because I hadn't wanted to ensnare her in her son's love triangle. I'd chosen to trust Phillip. I'd willingly given my heart to him. So, the pains I was feeling were my own fault for playing the role of a fool.

His mother advised me that she wasn't certain where Phillip stood but she was aware that he and his wife were talking. She thought possibly they were trying to reconcile. She also advised me that they'd always had a rocky marriage yet, always managed to get back together. These words fell hard in my ears; they crushed what little spirit I had left. His mother explained that this had been their longest separation and no other children had been born outside the marriage.

Phillip was quite surprised to see his belongings packed. He tried to pretend I was over re-acting but I refused to be patronized. Mama always taught me that if I were to do anything, to do it right. I knew she'd be greatly disappointed if she knew of the pit I'd allowed myself to fall in. But, I wasn't insisting Phillip leave now rather than later because of what Mama would think. I was doing it for myself. Phillip would not sneak out on me like a thief in the night. I don't really think it was so much a pride issue, he'd made his decision. It was simply the right thing to do.

I assume he moved back home--his home--with his wife and children. A couple of weeks later, Phillip dropped by to see Amber. As he was leaving, we were standing on the porch talking when his eldest daughters' friend walked by gawking in amazement between us and his car. It was as though she'd found a great treasure. Later that evening, Phillips' wife began cruising by my home, assumedly searching for his car. Since he had a child who lived there, sometimes she'd find it. Phillip was dedicated to supporting his children--all his children. He constantly tried to rekindle the fire that had never died. Though the coals still smoldered, the flames could not ignite as the damper had been permanently shut off. It was not that I didn't love him, I still do. But, I loved myself more. I loved my children more, more than to teach them this way of life.

Angered by finding Phillip's car in my driveway, his wife threw rocks and bricks breaking my windows. Ironically, he'd then have to spend more time there repairing the damage. She'd call me, cursing and threatening me. She seemed to take pleasure in renaming me every four or five letter ill-conceived word imaginable. She had words I'd never heard before, and certainly not directed at myself. Her children began calling at all times asking for my daughter, Twyla. They were eager to practice their great inheritance of using foul language and junior threats. Of course, after recognizing their voices and realizing they were not Twyla's friends, they were not permitted to speak to her.

Many times Phillip's wife threatened to kill me. She told me she was going to shoot me and no one would ever find out she was the guilty party. She was going to pour gasoline around my home, strike a match to it and burn me and my 'bastard baby' up. It appeared to give her great comfort to discuss her plans with me. She'd call every two or three hours until the wee hours of the morning. The only reason I continued to answer the phone was because it could have been something of importance. This was before having the option of caller ID. I wondered how she managed to work a forty hour shift given all the telephone extra-curricular activities she was putting in.

I was curt with her but never rude. It was not a part of my make-up. Besides, I knew I'd been wrong. God had blessed me with the ability to feel another's pain, to understand other's point-of-view even if it differed than my own. I was confused by why she spent so much time attempting to harass me when Phillip and I were no longer together. I wondered why she didn't spend that time more constructively--like, rebuilding her marriage.

One whole month passed and her telephone harassment continued. I'd changed my phone number to an unlisted one and within days, she'd obtained the new number. She called to laugh at me saying I couldn't get away from her and boasted of having friends who worked for the telephone company. Then, the threats started again. The police could do nothing; they claimed no physical crime had been committed. I'm sure harassment laws have changed now to include threats via telephone.

Meanwhile, it had begun to wear on me. I was extremely tired from being awakened several times during the night. I was still functioning normally. I took care of my children, went to work daily, cleaned my house and cooked. As I drove to work every day for that month, Jesus sat in the passenger seat of my car. The drive took twenty minutes, and for twenty minutes, Jesus was my silent passenger. I didn't see Him with my physical eye, but I felt His presence. His presence was far stronger than any natural body. I felt I could've reached over and touched Him. Precious few things are sacred, and I knew Jesus was. Holy. Jesus is Holy. It was not an option to attempt to touch Him with unclean hands.

I'd willingly gotten myself tangled into this web. Sometimes Jesus will get you out of your web and sometimes He'll get into the web with you. Although He did not approve of my decisions, He climbed into the web with me, giving me the strength I needed to move forward. I'd turned my back on God, had deliberately walked against His perfect will. I'd committed the sin of adultery, which is warned against in the Ten Commandments. But, God still recognized me as His child. Jesus still came to me in a time of crisis.

I prayed and asked God for forgiveness and for this ordeal to be over. Shortly thereafter, Phillip came over one evening unexpectedly. The phone rang just as I'd let him in and I went to answer it. Phillip followed me into the kitchen. His wife was on the telephone. This time, she was actually being decent.

"Well, girl, are you tired yet?" she asked.

"Yes, I really am," I replied.

She laughed softly. Evidently she was tired herself. Then, she made the remark that I needed to quit wasting my time with Phillip because he didn't want me.

"Hold on," I said and passed the phone to Phillip. Not realizing who was on the line, he answered. I snickered at the steady stream of vulgarity that rang in his ears. She was yelling so loudly, I could hear her from where I was standing. Phillip said about two words to her and hung the phone up.

Shaking his head and looking teasingly at me, he said: "You know you're wrong."

I laughed. "She shouldn't be calling over here! We're not together anymore. You're the one who made those vows to her--and broke them. Her problem lies with you, not me."

Evidently, she had other ideas. Within thirty minutes, she was beating on my door. It was summer. I'd left the wooden door open and the screen pulled up. Phillip and I were still sitting around the kitchen table talking and my children were asleep since it was past their bedtime. From the kitchen doorway, I could see the anger blazing in her eyes. She knocked repeatedly as I was on my way to the door. Phillip came up behind me and she filled my neighborhood with such foul language as to cause the devil to be glorified. Her children were waiting in the car. She called out to them, saying, "Come help me beat this bitch up." Giving honor to their mother, they came running to aid her. All four of them stood there calling me names and flagrantly tossing out every curse word that came to their minds. Phillip was appalled, disgusted, and hurt. I doubt he'd ever actually seen or heard his children cussing like sailors before. He stood in front of me and told them to go home. His wife became even more enraged.

"You taking up for this bitch?" she exclaimed in hot anger. "Well, I'll take care of that! I'll kill the bitch!" She ran to her car, came back with a revolver and burst through the door like the police. Phillip grabbed her hand that held the gun. They wrestled until he was able to take it from her and force her outside. He shut the wooden door and I called the police. Angry that they were all on my front porch giving my neighbors a free movie, I peeped outside at them. She was still trying to take the gun from Phillip and her mouth never failed to flow its filth. I called the police again. I wondered how it was that a woman so petite and pretty could allow such ugliness to live within her soul. No wonder Phillip can't stay with her for any length of time, I thought. Then, I realized that I was just giving him an excuse.

I continued to peep outside watching the drama unfold on my front porch. Phillip had one of his daughters lock the gun in the trunk of her car as he tried to reason with his wife. He told her she should not have the children involved in this type situation. Up in his face like and angry setting hen, she was far too bitter to be reasoned with.

"It seems to me like your friend could've picked out someone better than this! So, what you gonna do? You gonna to stay over here in this rent house with this bitch and her bastard baby or you gonna come home with your family?" she asked.

I knew I was seeing her at her worst. I knew she had every right to be consumed with anger. I tried, but I couldn't make myself become angry with her even at this point. Though I had not walked in her shoes, I knew where she was coming from. From her comments about the house and our meeting, I also knew that she could've only obtained this information through Phillip.

It took three calls before the police arrived. They talked to us separately. One officer spoke to her and her children, another to Phillip and me. I suppose they felt the need to immediately separate Phillip from his wife until some of the fire died down. They did not arrest her even though she'd brandished a gun. Their reasoning for the non-arrest was that this was 'a family matter and no harm was done.' I suppose she would've really needed to have killed me in order to be arrested. The police took my complaint, escorted Phillip, his wife and children off my property and advised me that I should not be involved with a married man.

Oh, what wisdom lies in those sworn to protect and to serve. Yes, that is sarcasm.

I prayed long and hard that night. I thanked God for allowing my daughters to sleep through this ugliness. I thanked Him for preventing further violence. I asked Him to remove my stumbling block. I prayed for strength to face my coming tomorrows. I prayed for Phillip's happiness. I prayed for peace.

Five days later, Phillip and his family moved to Denver, Colorado. I don't know how long they'd planned it. I just know that five days later—they moved. Peace was restored to my home.

When I drove to work on Monday, my heart was full but my passenger seat was vacant. Jesus had weathered the long and turbulent storm with me. He hadn't left me defenseless in the war I'd helped to ignite. The war was now over and He'd moved His holy presence to assist others whose storms were raging out of control.

"Except the Lord build the house,
they labor in vain that build it."
Psalm 127:1

"If my people,
which are called by my name, shall humble themselves,
and pray, and seek my face, and turn from their wicked ways;
Then will I hear from heaven, and will forgive their sin,
and will heal their land." II Chronicles 7: 14

Lois Snell

A Comforter Is Sent

Chapter 12

On the night Phillip and I broke up, I was deeply disturbed. I'd been the picture of strength and determination during the conversation. Now, he was gone and I'd retrieved my key. My daughters were sleeping peacefully and I could be honest with myself. The only way I'd found to hold onto my strength and sanity was to choose my down times carefully--out of view of my children. As they tasted the sweetness of slumber, I allowed my body to release the pain trapped inside.

I was scheduled for testing for one of the post office positions the following morning. Naturally, I didn't want my distress to show on my face nor in my scores. After the sobs had not subsided in what was ample time, I became anxious of tomorrows test. A quick trip to the bathroom mirror confirmed that I was in deep trouble. Certainly, my eyes would be swollen and red of tears. Finally, I drifted off to sleep shortly after midnight.

Awakened by the sunshine beaming down on my face, I stirred and glanced at the clock. It read three fifteen and I was confused and alarmed by the lateness of the hour. Surely I couldn't have slept all day, I thought. That would mean my daughters had as well. I hadn't prepared breakfast or lunch and, I'd missed out on my opportunity for the all-important postal test. Something was certainly wrong if the three of us had slept all night and the majority of the day as well. I attempted to go check on my daughters but was confronted with both lightness and darkness--two worlds in my room.

My room was just as it'd been before I'd fallen asleep. It was dark with only a faint glow from the bathroom light filtering in. The deep pine dresser was in its rightful place. The closet doors were closed.

Nothing was in array on my night table. The blue and white eyelet bedspread gently covered my body and gracefully hung toward the floor. It was my room--in the deep of night. Yet, inside my room, another world—down home with the brightness of midday—rested within its walls.

Acres upon acres of down home splendor were illuminated in my room. I felt the warm but gentle breeze while watching the fields of golden wheat swaying beautifully in tune. I lay there, in my bed, looking at both worlds at the same time in total amazement.

The old folks used to say, "Honey, I was having such a good time, I pinched myself to make sure I was there." I'd always thought that statement was so ridiculous, so country and so contrived. But, that night, I pinched myself to make certain I was there. In the darkness, I felt the pain of the pinch just as surely as I'd felt the warmth of the sunshine beaming down on my face.

In the distance, on the top of the big hill, a horse and rider appeared. The horse was in full gallop as he descended the big hill then the smaller one. As he came closer, I recognized the rider as Daddy Crook. The horse entered our yard and reared up on his hind legs at the edge of the porch, which was also the edge of my bed. Daddy dismounted and tied the horse to the wooden post. I lay in my bed staring at this huge horse and wondering how he could so easily fit inside my room. To my further amazement, I came out of our home wearing the yellow and black striped short set I'd made in Home Economics during my senior year.

There she was again--the other Lois--in the same place at the same time as I was. This time, we were worlds apart and she appeared younger by several years than my then current age. She was very much the girl that had grown up in the house she'd just come out of. Neither she nor Daddy was aware of my lying in bed watching them in wonder. They appeared to be confined to their realm. The other Lois was extremely happy to see Daddy. Although she was younger, perhaps seventeen years, she was aware that Daddy had been deceased by several years. This tragedy happened when she would've been older yet she knew of the details of their deaths. Also, she seemed to know events from my current life.

Her heart, my heart, overflowed at the sight of Daddy alive, well and happy with no gunshot wounds. The other Lois and I were two in body but one in spirit. I felt all the emotions she felt. We ran into his open arms and he held her--us--while we cried. He comforted us with his presence, not with words. When our tears were spent, he looked into our eyes. He saw and felt our pain of losing Phillip. Daddy's comfort was for my current problems, not that of the young lady of my past. He knew all the answers to our unasked questions. He knew our future, our destiny, as well as that of my daughters and their children yet to be born. He knew everything that was to come.

The other Lois and I saw the wisdom in his eyes. We knew he had ready answers to any question we'd ask. We also saw through his eyes that he was under commission of God and was not to divulge our future. He was sent only to comfort. Without questioning, without doubt, this, we knew.

Daddy specifically asked how one of my older cousins was doing as we sat down on the edge of the porch.

"She's fine."

He then inquired about another cousin. I explained that she was fine also. Daddy already knew how they were doing just as he'd known how I was doing. He was deliberately diverting my focus off myself and placing it on others. At leisure, we discussed everyone in the family. Abruptly, he stood up and I naturally followed him. Without either saying a word, we knew it was time for him to leave. Sad that he was leaving, I hugged him again.

"Daddy, I hate you have to go so soon. It was so good to see you." We meant that in every sense of the words. Our last image of Daddy Crook was as he'd lain in a coffin, void of life. Our minds held images of the pain he'd felt being shot with his own shotgun while asleep. Though we knew he never saw his murderer, he surely felt the pain of that shotgun blast. To see him moving in his old strength, alive, vibrant and happy was more than words could express. Daddy was concerned about events in our lives just as he'd been during his lifetime. This was more than a miracle.

Daddy nodded and untied the horse. "Lois, in any given situation, you shouldn't be the only one to say I love you."

Although we had not discussed my relationship with Phillip, I knew that was what Daddy was referring to. Phillip had spoken the words, but his words had never carried the weight or depth mine had. Of course, I knew that Phillip did love me--the person I was. I knew he respected me and wanted his future with me. And, I knew that he wanted to want these things. But, loving a person and wanting to love a person are worlds apart from being in love with a person. Phillip was in love with his wife. Deep down, I knew that. Otherwise, he would've been able to distance himself from the problematic marriage and not allow threats of extremely high child support payments to sway his decision. While we were together, there'd been a few times I'd secretly observed Phillip sitting quietly, deeply in thought. During those times, there was sadness about him I knew I couldn't reach. I could not define it in words nor could I rationalize it in thought.

When Daddy was ready to mount, he looked at me and said, "Lois, I'm here whenever you need me."

At that very moment, it was as though someone threw a brick into a large mirror. The vision of Daddy Crook, the other Lois, the horse and acres of sunlit down home splendor broke into large pieces. The shattered pieces began to float in the air and become smaller. In the space of moments, they continued to shrink and became particles as fine as dust, then disappeared altogether. All that was left was the darkness of my room as it'd been before.

"All you have to do, is call out to me," Daddy Crook's voice said from the nothingness.

I've shared this vision with many people and they've generally found it difficult to believe. It is phenomenal. I was witness to it, a participant in it and, even I studied the vision for years in wonderment.

Then I remembered the Scripture of Psalm 24: 1, "The earth is the Lord's, and the fullness thereof; the world, and they that dwell therein." The world is God's and the fullness thereof. The body, the spirit is given of God into the world. They belong to Him. Mortal men have no power to quicken the spirit, to hold on to something as dear as breath once life has passed. They have no power to restore themselves regardless to how noble the cause may be. Jesus, the Christ, is the only one that was bestowed with that great honor. Men are human and are born and die. They do not become angels with messages to deliver.

Yet, I can think of no one or nothing that could've offered me more comfort than my Daddy Crook who raised, loved and comforted me during his lifetime. When my heart was wounded, I didn't need crying rocks or talking donkeys to comfort me. I wouldn't have warmed up to them. Therefore, the comfort and peace sent from God would've eluded me, plunging me into deeper despair.

I had been spiritual all my life, had seen visions and heard voices all my life. God knows all our weakness' and strengths. He knows our breaking points. He knows what image to send, when to send it and where to send it. He knows everything. I've come to believe that God manifested the Holy Spirit in the likeness of my Daddy Crook to offer me the comfort I needed. I've come to believe this because, even during the vision, the characteristics Daddy Crook held were that of Deity--knowledge of all things, omnipresent.

"And I will pray the Father,
and he shall give you another
Comforter
that he may abide with you
forever;
Even the spirit of truth;
whom the world cannot receive
because it seeth him not,
neither knoweth him:
but ye know him;
for he dwelleth with you,
and shall be in you.
I will not leave you comfortless;
I will come to you."
John 14:16-18

Live Wires, The Death Of Phillip

Chapter 13

Phillip's reconciliation lasted three weeks, he claimed. Four months later, he returned to Oklahoma. Shortly thereafter, he called wanting to see Amber. It was not my right, nor was it my desire to keep a child from her father. Yet, somewhere deeply within my heart, I felt he deserved some type of punishment. The evils inside me wanted his daughter to have completely wiped him from her memory. Their bond was too strong. Amber had been napping in her crib when he'd come to visit her. Hearing his voice in the living room, she awoke. She screamed with excitement when he walked into her bedroom. Grabbing the handrails, she bounced higher than ever in the crib until he'd taken her.

Phillip held her closely, kissing her cheeks and playing with her curly ringlets while she laughed and screamed of joy. The scene warmed my heart. Discerning that I'd wanted her to reject him, he looked at me smugly. I'd been silently convicted of my unspoken crime.

Phillip wasted no time in trying to patch things up with me. He apologized for leaving and willingly shared slices of his life in Denver. I advised him that I wasn't interested in his life but he insisted on pleading his case anyway. I listened half-heartedly, pretending I was less interested than I actually was. It was not an option for us to be together; but, because I loved him, I did want him in a happy and stable relationship--free of anger and violence.

He had many stories to share. My senses perked up when he shared of an experience with a man he'd met in Denver who was gifted with sight. The man prophesied Phillip's death. Of course, I didn't believe this. I wasn't certain if he actually believed it or was using it to try to lure me into another forbidden trap. By now, Phillip's credibility with me was null and void. The person he'd met told him he could see an aura around him. The man explained that previously when he'd seen an aura around others, they'd died shortly thereafter. I'd never known anyone with the ability to see impending death and warn others so they may set their house in order. I wasn't certain how I should deal with this information. I couldn't refer to it as knowledge. Phillip always told me that he hadn't expected to live to reach age thirty-five. I'd equated that fear with his running the streets during his younger years. He was more settled now, young and healthy; I saw no reason why his life should end abruptly. We talked at length about many things.

The love I felt for Phillip had not died. But, the old adage is true--God puts one's eyes in front of their faces to see where they're going--not where they've been. Mama and Daddy had always taught us to move forward. As much as I loved Phillip, I couldn't move forward in a backwards situation. His family had faces now. They were not some foreign entity that I knew existed out there, somewhere. They had recognizable faces, voices and personalities--far different than my own, yet tangible.

Without my admitting it, Phillip knew I still loved him. He knew what he was asking was unfair and unrealistic. He knew his life was not his own. Yet, the facts didn't prevent him from trying. As time passed, he realized I couldn't be swooned into the same snare and he found another love interest. Earnestly, I wished him happiness and peace. Our lines of communication never died.

I'd been without employment for several months and it appeared that no job was soon to be found. I was either over qualified or under qualified for everything I applied for and no one was willing to launch out in faith. McDonalds even rejected me. Along with employment, privileges began to disappear. The telephone had been disconnected for four months. On February nineteenth, Saturday evening at four o'clock I'd just finished sweeping the kitchen floor. I'd stooped to sweep the trash into the dustpan when the telephone rang. I stood straight up and looked at it in surprise. From the telephone, I glanced to the clock. This was really weird. When the phone rang again, I answered it.

Phillip's voice was on the other end, asking to speak to his eldest daughter, specifically calling her by name. I advised him he had the wrong number. Immediately recognizing Phillip's voice, I wondered why he hadn't recognized mine. I hang the phone up and returned to my chores. The phone rang again and I answered wondering how in the world it was possible. It was a clear day with no rains in the forecast. No snow, no ice. Therefore, inclement weather could not be credited to the ringing of deadlines. Sure enough, it was Phillip again asking for his daughter who was about eighteen years of age. Amber was just past two so he definitely had dialed the wrong number.

"No one by that name lives here," I added giving him more time to catch my voice and realize his error. Certain he'd dialed the right number, he asked for her again. "Wrong number," I said, then listened to the silence before hanging up.

I emptied the dustpan and the telephone rang again. This time when I picked it up, the line was live, then went dead. No click, no buzz, just dead. For the rest of the evening, I kept looking at the phone in wonder. That night, I had fitful sleep. I kept waking up expecting the phone to ring and Phillip to be on the other end. I suppose I hoped it would ring again so I could talk to him. I wanted to tell him whose number he'd actually dialed. I tossed and turned for the better part of the night, longing to talk to Phillip—about anything.

The following morning, Charlene came over to advise me that Phillip had been killed the previous evening. Unable to reach me by phone, his mother called her to relay the message. Charlene intentionally did not deliver the message that night because she didn't want me to have to cope with this alone. Around six o'clock, Phillip had been shot while trying to stop a fight between his nephew and his niece's boyfriend. He'd deliberately jumped into the line of fire to prevent his nephew from being killed. Phillip died in transit to the hospital about six thirty.

I realized the telephone calls were God's way of warning me of impending doom.

My heart felt torn, empty--yet still bleeding. I sat there in shock and hurt for some time. My sister sat with me, we didn't talk. She stayed, silently trying to absorb some of the pain I felt. Phillip's death seemed altogether untimely and was--so final.

But, I needed to feed my children. I needed to comb their hair, to make their beds and make sure they had their baths that night. I needed to gather them in my arms and tell them I loved them. I needed to kiss them and hold them tightly. I needed to prepare Twyla for school on Monday. I needed to talk with God. I needed to plead for his grace and mercy to allow me to live to raise my daughters, to see them educated and secure in their own right. It was not an option to fall apart.

Lois Snell

"And God shall wipe away
all tears from their eyes;
and there shall be no more death,
neither sorrow, nor crying,
neither shall there be any more pain:
for the former things
have passed away."
Revelation 21:4

Saved From Demons

Chapter 14

The luxury of rest had escaped me for three weeks straight as I could only sleep for two or three hours at a time. Between the hours of two and three in the morning, I'd awaken suddenly for no apparent reason. Then, I'd lie awake for a couple of hours. Aside of medication, I'd tried everything to be able to sleep throughout the night, but nothing worked. Having examined my problems, I felt I was coping with them as well as possible. I was still seeking employment. Phillip's death, six months prior, still brought pains to my heart which was normal. But, I felt the disturbance in my sleep was not connected to his death, nor my problems, financial worries or stress. I'd gone to bed extra late yet still woke within a few hours. Reserving my chores until later in hopes of tiring myself out proved unbeneficial. I'd always been a light sleeper, but this was rather ridiculous. Both confused and concerned about my inability to sleep, I often asked God why to no avail.

Since we live in the "now" generation, most of us find it very difficult to wait for answers when God is silent. We've come to expect everything quickly. Not only do hours and minutes matter to us, seconds do. Instead of attempting to push rush orders on God, we should use quiet restraint and pray for patience as we wait. During the times we feel God is silent, He is very likely already paving the way that will benefit us most.

Charlene called me very early one Sunday morning quite alarmed over a dream she'd had. In her dream, my daughters and I were involved in a tragic accident that ended in my death. The images were extremely vivid and powerful; they frightened her to the point of calling. She warned me to be careful and we talked at length, yet she was not comforted by the time we'd finished. I thanked her for sharing the dream and told her I'd be fine. After all, my car had engine problems and was not movable. It was not possible to become involved in an accident in it.

Mozella Harrison, my best friend, called on Thursday of that same week. She also called to discuss a frightening dream with me. Mozella is a police officer. In her dream, she was cruising down Martin Luther King Boulevard and was asked to respond to a traffic accident that had just occurred. As she approached the scene, she recognized my brown and white Dodge Challenger. With a sinking heart, she began to assess the damage as she drove up. Shaken but alive, my children were standing on the shoulder of the street while I'd not fared as well. Lifeless, my body lay sprawled in the street drenched in blood. Mozella was very concerned about the dream and warned me repeatedly to be careful. I thanked her for sharing her dream and told her she need not worry as the Challenger wasn't running. For the second time in four days, I reiterated that it was impossible to become involved in an accident in the Challenger.

One week later, I awoke at three o'clock in the morning. Immediately, I felt this strange, uncomfortable and overwhelming pressure from my lower ribcage throughout my chest. As I'd lain asleep, a demon apparently had entered my body. It started talking to me. Although I assumed it to be speaking from within, I could hear it plainly through my ear as though it lay beside me. This is a paradox. I've been told that Satan's demons can't possess a Christian. The feeling of pressure from the inside and hearing the demon's voice from the outside would seem to suggest that he was on the outside and exerting pressure to make me feel as though I'd consumed it. Nothing was visible to the eye.

"Come on, let's go for a ride," It said in a smooth, relatively soft voice.

I was in total shock. I'd never witnessed the presence of evil before and, at that very moment, I wasn't certain it was evil. I'd seen visions and heard voices throughout my lifetime. They'd always been loving, protective and guiding--instruments of comfort, instruments of light. I felt uncomfortable with this. Uncomfortable, even though he spoke softly in my right ear. I'd always equated Satan with being on one's left since the Scriptures state plainly that Jesus sits at the right hand of God. In my mind, I'd always envisioned Jesus on the right side of anything. However, we should never attempt to contain God, Jesus, nor the Holy Spirit to any physical geographic area. They are everywhere at all times.

Satan is most vile and cunning. He uses everything you've ever imagined or held to be truth against you. In my dazed state, newly awakened from much needed sleep, it would've been easy to be deceived into assuming this message was from Jesus, the risen Christ.

"No," I answered not knowing to whom I was speaking.

"Come on. It's a nice day for a ride," It said.

Memories of Charlene and Mozella's dreams were suddenly ablaze in my mind and I quickly equated "ride" with death.

"No, I don't want to go," I said.

"Sure you do. You haven't been out in a while. The air is nice and fresh. It's a good day for a ride. Come on."

"No," I said feeling very uncomfortable from both the pressure in my chest and the realization that this was not of God. God does not haggle with us. He asks but He does not coerce. He gives us directions followed by free will.

"Lois, admit it. You're tired. You're worried about the future; you're worried about the bills. You're worried that you won't have enough food. Right now, you're worried about paying the electric bill. You're under a lot of stress. I'm offering you freedom from all that. Come on," the demon said.

"No," I said lying perfectly still. It did sound good. So good! I was extremely tired of worrying about the bills all the time. There was never enough money. Stress had moved in with me and set up camp. But, somehow I knew that if I moved even a fraction of an inch, I would be gone--forever.

"No more worries. Perfect peace. Come on."

"No, my car doesn't work," I answered feeling as though I had to justify my decision.

"It'll work," the demon of Satan spoke with assurance. "All you have to do is lay your hand on it."

At that moment, my hand--my right hand--simply oozed of power. It was as though it were gloved with all the electric power of the world. If I'd wanted fifty million dollars, I need only to slightly move the tip of my little finger and it'd be mine for the taking. I knew that. What's more, I wouldn't have to pick it up or do any labor for it. Whatever I wanted would be made available. So, getting the car started, like Satan's demon said, would pose no problem.

"No, I can't go. I can't leave my kids."

"You don't have to leave them. Put them in the car with you. You don't want other people mistreating them, feeding their kids and not yours. Sending them to school with uncombed hair. Come on, Lois. Take the kids with you. We'll all go for a ride."

Now, that made me *MAD!* It was one thing for Satan to attempt to coerce me into death. But, he was not about to talk me into killing my children. By now, I knew I was dealing with Satan. He is a smooth talking, power provoking liar whose greatest weapon is the power of suggestion. I was no match for him. The lives of my children were at stake. At this very moment, he was using my love as a mother to try to defeat me. Using words and imagery I'd always feared or hated. He knew that one of my pet peeves was seeing children with uncombed hair. And, to add sending them to school like that was totally unacceptable.

At first light of realizing you're speaking to or dealing with Satan, you must cease communication at once. Every word, every thought, every emotion expended puts you at risk for destruction.

He sensed my anger and revulsion and knew he'd struck a wrong chord with me. I felt his hand on my left shoulder trying to pull me up. Now, he had no power to pull: I just felt the pressure of his hand and that was more coercion for me to move. Just as he had no power to force Eve to eat the fruit in the Garden of Eden, he is still limited to the power of persuasion. His hold over mankind is limited to what we allow our minds to receive as fact and if we allow our bodies to act out his will rather than God's. Don't take this lightly. Satan's power of persuasion is masterfully crafted. It's so strong, you'll often feel as though you're acting out your own will. He'll reason with you and make perfect sense at the time. So, you must be watchful of his tactics. Remember Jesus' words, watch and pray.

I'm not certain that this will hold true in all cases, but when I'd finally recognized Satan for whom he is, he was on the left side where I felt he belonged. Maybe this is another ploy of his to keep me confused.

He's also a spirit, an evil spirit, with free range. Don't go to bed without being prayed up. He even attacks you when you're asleep.

"Oh God, help me please!" I cried aloud.

At that very moment, Satan was gone. My cry to God for help was all that was needed. I didn't feel his leaving just as I hadn't felt his coming but, the pressure was gone from my chest and no smooth talking words were coming from the air. God had saved me from demons. My God--the One, True and Living God--had saved me from Satan's demons!

Know where your source of strength and protection comes from. It's from the Holy One who rules throughout eternity. He is the only power, the only entity that has the power not only to save your life, but to save your soul. God, Almighty! Praise to His name forever.

Fearful and crying, I jumped out of bed and ran into my children's room. I was thirty-one years old and strong in my faith. If demons could have such influence over me, I wondered what they could do to mere children who hadn't the time to grow into their deep faith of God. Children are defenseless, they may not be able to totally appreciate and accept the fact that Jesus is the Christ who died for our sins and was raised up on the third day to live throughout eternity.

Satan's coercion and lies have never ceased. He offers money, power and possessions but ultimately delivers death and destruction. His lies have only grown stronger and more cunning. This is the very reason you hear of decent, loving people suddenly killing their families and themselves. It's because Satan and his demons smooth-talked them into it. They've had thousands of years of practice since Eve was beguiled. The demons used every trick they'd learned to lure those souls unto death before they'd realized that even a frantic plea to God would've saved their lives. Just call him--"Jesus!" He is faithful and just to hear your calls. Jesus will come to your aid before the second syllable hits your tongue.

Suddenly, it became clear why I'd been awakened at night for three weeks prior to this. He attacks when you're unsuspecting and unprepared. Satan's demon had been trying to influence me all the time. God knew I was not strong enough to recognize him for what he is--a thief, a liar, a murderer and a deceiver of souls. So, God chose to wake me up before Satan could destroy me. God chose to send my sister and my friend the frightening dreams depicting the future of what Satan planned. My God stirred the emotions in both Charlene and Mozella to the point that they had to discuss their worst fears with me. Not only did they need to discuss them, they had to deposit in my subconscious nature a very real fear. God chose those closest to me as vessels of light sailing across a darkened sea. Some dreams aren't meant to be kept to oneself. Those were not ordinary dreams. They were warnings, visions sent from Almighty God that greatly aided in saving my life. In fact, those visions may be solely responsible for my being able to write these memoirs today. If memory had not flicked---

I kneeled down between my children's twin beds and took each of their hands. They were sleeping so peacefully. I cried and pleaded with God to deliver my family from evil. I begged that Satan would not have dominion over us. I prayed that my children would walk in God's light and that He would place a hedge of protection around them. I was there on my knees, weeping and holding their hands for a very long time. I was trying to let my faith and trust in God filter into them. After my prayer ended, I pushed their beds together. I lay between them and pulled them to me letting their heads rest on my shoulders. They didn't even stir during my long prayer and repositioning of their beds. With my arms of love and protection wrapped around their small bodies, I fell asleep in prayer.

I thank God for conquering the future before it became a reality. I thank Him for His grace and wisdom, His undying love. I thank Him for having encamped angels around my family to protect us from evil. They are also encamped around yours.

Never feel that your life is so dull, so un-inspiring, that Satan wouldn't waste any time trying to lure you into destruction. Your life is not comprised solely of the number of breaths you take. It's viewed in the long run, your children, your grandchildren and your entire lineage. Your living and breathing now affects their outcome and every family has greatness in its midst. Your life also affects the hundreds of thousands of others you'll come in contact with and ultimately be able to influence in some way. Your life has value, great value. Jesus thought of you as He chose to be nailed to the cross. I thank Jesus for coming to Earth for me, for dying on the cross for sins I'd yet commit. I praise Him and thank Him for loving me enough to go to the cross for me. Isn't it amazing that He died for our sins, and now lives to protect us from those same sins? Jesus is the Christ, the only person, the only entity that could've taken on this great commission. He is worthy to be praised!

If you receive nothing more from this chapter, I need you to receive that you can never let your guard down with Satan. He attacks you even during your sleep. Don't go to sleep unprotected by prayer. If he manages to slither himself into your life, even in dreams, take charge over the situation by crying out to God for help. You have the power to banish Satan from your presence, but that power only lies in the cry to God for help. God is faithful and just. Rely on him. I bear witness that demons flee from the presence of God. They flee from the sound of His name! Call Him.

"He delivered me from my strong enemy,
and from them which hated me:
for they were too strong for me."
Psalm 18:17

Jesus In My Room

Chapter 15

I slept in the room with my children for the next three months. and prayed faithfully every night, making sure my daughters did so as well. They were not aware of why I slept there and assumed we simply enjoyed camping out together. Blessed sleep had been restored since my battle with Satan's demon.

Christmas was quickly approaching and I was still unemployed. My rainy day funds had washed away with the flood. Still, God made provisions for us.

The ten o'clock news showcased a family that had recently relocated to Oklahoma City. The father's job had gone sour within weeks of his arrival and the family was now homeless. The family included the father, mother, a daughter slightly younger than Twyla, and a toddler son. They were living in the Jesus House, a recluse for homeless people. My heart turned with compassion for the little blonde headed girl who, when asked what she wanted for Christmas, responded with "a nice warm coat."

Looking around at the beauty and warmth of my surroundings, I realized how blessed I was. I'd been unemployed for one year and, through the grace of God, we'd not been displaced. I'd staggered the bills. One month we may have been without electricity, a few months later, gas. When the electricity was off, I lit an oil lamp and told my daughters this was how I'd once studied for school. I cooked on the grill and told them interesting stories in lieu of their watching television. We actually enjoyed those times. It served as a learning experience for them and, strangely enough, we grew even closer as a family.

Going through rough times is often accredited to the breakdown of families. That should not be. We all will experience rough times at some point in our lives. The evil one targets families for destruction. Once he's successfully destroyed the family structure, it's easier for him to destroy individual lives. He uses the oldest trick in the world, divide and conquer. "The Lord is mighty in battle." (Psalms 24:8) If the will of God is kept in our hearts during our most troublesome battles, nothing can tear our families apart.

The family shown on the news bothered me to the point of my wanting to help them. I didn't offer shelter for two reasons. The first was that I didn't trust strangers with my children. Secondly, I wasn't exactly sure I'd have shelter payment next month. Yet, I was compelled to do something so I went into Twyla's closet, filled a garbage bag with clothes, shoes and a nice warm coat for the little girl. These were not shabby clothing. They were lovely items, some of which Twyla was still wearing. Some that still had price tags connected to them. You don't offer a hungry child an empty plate. Likewise, I gathered a garbage bag full from my closet for the mother and sat the two bags by the living room door. Charlene would be coming by the next day. She dropped by every few days to see if I needed to go to the grocery store or run errands. I intended to ask her to drop the bags off at the Jesus House for me.

My sister, Ivy, supplied my closets with beautiful clothing. She knew I'd always worked hard and had little left after bills were paid. Ivy also knew that I kept my daughters looking like little dolls and spent virtually nothing on myself. Therefore, she made it her mission to keep me clothed in beauty. I never asked anything of anyone but, Ivy was determined to aid in keeping my spirits high. At least once or twice a year, she'd send two large boxes filled with leather purses, scarves, shoes and clothes, both casual and dressy. On more than one occasion, she deliberately went to the shopping malls and shopped for me. She wanted to give me an edge on securing a good paying job by making sure my attire was not a deterrent. It was her gift of love. God does work in mysterious ways and those ways often include using the hands of others.

I'd fallen fast asleep on the night of the troubling newscast. I was awakened suddenly for no apparent reason. I glanced at the clock, two in the morning. My battle with demons came rushing back to my mind and I was paralyzed with fear.

Oh no, I thought. It's happening again!

With the exception of a crack for the night-light, the door to the hallway was always closed at night. I turned to make sure it was still closed. There was a portrait hanging on the wall that didn't belong there as the door remained open on a daily basis and would've blocked its view. No one decorates with fine portraits in a place where they cannot be appreciated.

In confusion, I studied the portrait. Inside its frame, I saw Jesus. As I looked inside the walls of the frame, I realized I was looking through the ages of time. Jesus was at the end of the tunnel. Years, generations, ages and worlds separated us.

"Jesus," I breathed.

Within a blink of an eye, Jesus was in my room. In full form, His whole body was glistening in my room. He'd traveled through the ages of time in less than a fraction of a second. His raiment was brilliantly white, billowing, highly illuminating. His head, stable and sure, hallowed in glory. His hair was a mass of dark waves hanging about his shoulders. His hands were strong and powerful, but gentle. And His eyes, they were filled with love. His presence--the very essence of His being illuminated the whole room with marvelous light.

I was already lying down, so I couldn't fall to my knees in awe. But, my whole body was humbled by His presence. My mouth fell open in sheer shock that He, Jesus, the Christ, the Son of God, the great I AM, would choose for whatever reason to manifest Himself in my presence. I wanted to talk to Him, to ask countless questions of Him, to obtain knowledge and understanding of many things. I knew this was a great and rare opportunity and there were seemingly hundreds of questions whirling around in my mind all at once.

"You look just like your pictures," is what came out of my mouth. Jesus smiled at me just as any loving father would do when his child said something humorous. His smile was of love, of warmth, of light and comfort. His eyes conveyed that I could go back to sleep now. They reassured me that He is the good Shepherd, and He does, indeed, watch over His sheep. He did not speak audibly to me; His eyes spoke to my soul. I breathed relief. Then, He was gone. The marvelous light that filled my room--gone. The time portrait on the wall was gone--the window of time, closed. But, the reassurance, comfort and peace I'd received from Jesus, Himself, would last a lifetime.

"I will not leave you comfortless:
I will come to you."
St. John 14:18

Lois Snell

"God, I Can't Die Now!"

Chapter 16

There was a terrible winter with snow and ice lasting for record periods of time. Parking lots of most companies were major hazards for their employees. That is, if they were fortunate enough to make it in to work. My work shift started at six o'clock in the morning. On this particular day, I hit a patch of black ice while in transit. My car was thrown into a tailspin over which I had no control. There were several sets of headlights in the rear view mirror. Not wanting others to become involved in the accident, I prayed they didn't catch up with me. Experience taught me that an accident was inevitable. My tire hit the curb, I could feel the car climb the embankment, both wheels were on the edge. I felt the wheels roll over.

"God, I can't die now! I still have the children to raise!" I cried.

My next memory was that of opening my eyes. *Well, I guess I'm still alive,* I thought while wiggling my fingers, then my toes. Their movement verified there were no broken bones. Memory surfaced of hitting the curb and my tires rolling over. Therefore, I realized I'd landed in the field that was approximately a forty foot drop from the street I'd been traveling on. Cars always exploded in the movies. I had to get out--and fast. Reaching for the door handle and pulling it as hard as possible was nightmarish as it didn't budge. Confused, I looked at it and saw the ground. That was when I realized the car had landed on its side. I tried to open the other door but its weight turned upside down was too strong for me.

Frantic, I noticed that the windshield was shattered, but not broken. With the side of my balled fist, I began to beat it. Knowing the car was a time bomb; I worked as quickly as I could. Certainly there were people on the street level who'd stopped to help me. They need not be involved in the explosion. I beat a hole in the windshield large enough to crawl through. Grabbing my purse, I climbed out to safety, hurriedly walking away but not before noticing the rear wheel was still rolling. I looked up toward the street to tell everyone I was fine and, to my amazement, no one was there. I closed my eyes and looked again because surely someone would've stopped. No one was there. On my hands and knees, I climbed up the snowy embankment until I'd reached street level. Once I'd reached the top, I looked down on my car and shivered at the thought of what could've happened. My car, lying in a field approximately forty feet below, was turned completely backwards from the direction in which I'd been traveling. I could have easily been crippled or killed. The fact was un-nerving. The sight was unbearable. I wondered if I weren't already dead and didn't know it. I had to move.

Charlene lived approximately two miles away. Knowing someone would give me a lift on this cold and snowy day, I proceeded to walk to her home. The bitterly cold wind was blowing in the direction I was walking and making good use of my face as target practice. Covered with glass from the windshield, I could feel little slivers of either glass or ice blowing into my eyes. I knew I'd go blind from this or, at least, have to wear glasses. I saw looks of horror, shock, compassion and indifference in the eyes of others as they met me and passed me by. Not one stopped to help or even to call a cab should they've been afraid.

Charlene was preparing to leave for work when I arrived. She dropped me off at my home. School had been canceled that day due to inclement weather. My daughters were deeply hurt by seeing me in such shabby condition. I told them I was fine and just needed to take a bath, wash my hair and rest. Wanting to comfort me in any way she could, Twyla ran my bath water. The warm water was soothing to both body and spirit. After emerging from its relaxing waters, I checked for damage and the only scratches found were on my hands from beating the windshield out.

I've mentally revisited this accident many times, raking through the ashes, searching for meaning. I was again working two jobs, including Sundays. Therefore, I'd fallen away from my deep commitment of attending church services on a weekly basis. In fact, I rarely ever attended. I remember standing on the ledge, looking down at my car in fear and trembling. It was then I realized this was God's way of telling me to go back--back to the point I'd left Him. I already knew God was my Deliverer, my Protector. The events surrounding this accident were a seal to that knowledge.

When I'm at the height of vulnerability, I place my trust in God. I called out to Him and, once again, He saved me from death.

"Behold, the eye of the Lord
is upon them that fear him,
upon them that hope in his mercy;
To deliver their soul from death,
and to keep them alive in famine.
Our soul waiteth for the Lord:
He is our help and our shield."
Psalm 33:18-20

Lois Snell

Letting Go Of Phillip

Chapter 17

Oftentimes, we give ourselves undeserved credit, unwarranted pats on the back for things we feel we've handled well. We even tell ourselves, I did this alone. In reality, we never do anything alone. We never do anything unless God permits it. For four years, I'd prided myself for handling Phillip's death with grace. This was not foolish pride that boasts, "Look at me, see how strong I am." It's the subtle pride that we don't realize is pride. The kind that simply keeps on going, keeps on doing what one thinks is right and proper. The kind that looks back every now and then and says, "I'm doing okay." That's the kind of pride I had.

Chills and fever awoke me in the midst of the night. I was babbling, talking in my sleep. I thought the words were random murmurings of the fever until they began to seep into my consciousness. I couldn't stop talking and I was now hearing what I was saying. I was talking to Phillip. Not to his spirit, not to his person, not going backwards in time. I was speaking into the wind, into the open air. Things that I'd long felt and never knew were there. I was angry with Phillip, angry with him for dying. I was angry with him for leaving me. Angrier still that he'd left me alone with now two small children to support. I was so angry with him--for dying.

Thus far, I had no idea I'd felt this sense of abandonment. I'd subconsciously kept it buried so deeply even the thought could not escape. Everything poured forth in my weakness. I spoke exactly what I felt about his dying--escaping from his responsibilities. I reminded him of the many times he'd promised to take care of his child. I called him a liar. I wanted him to hear me. I wanted to go stomp on his grave until he did. I wanted him to know how angry I was with him. He had no right to die.

After a time, the words of anger were spent. Anger is an emotion that was nearly foreign to me. Anger--the unseen force I'd bottled up inside had dissipated. I suddenly felt free of a heavy burden. By recognizing and acknowledging my true feelings, I was letting go of Phillip. Sleep came.

By morning, my fever had broken. My body was alight and alive with promise. I looked forward to my tomorrows. I was free.

Many times we prolong our mourning. So intent on being strong, I did this far too long. It's vitally important we realize that when a person slips from this realm of life, it's not by chance. It's because he has fulfilled the purposes for which he was born. God, and only He, assigns those purposes. Whether your loved ones are taken suddenly and without warning or have battled a long and painful illness, their days were numbered before they were born. Their death was not untimely. Their lifespan has come and gone just as was ordered by the Holy One. So, feel the pain--and let it go.

That sounds harsh, I know. You can't force yourself to grieve, or to complete the cycle of grief before it's time. But, in the interest of being strong, whether for others or for yourself, don't deny yourself the cleansing benefits of releasing pent-up anxieties that are better left to the wind. Our lives are never so connected with others that our purposes for living should be dulled, delayed or die due to their absence. God has designed specific purposes and meaning for all His children. As long as there are unresolved issues in our personal lives, we bind our hands from doing God's good work.

"I must work the works
of him that sent me,

while it is day:
the night cometh,
when no man can work."
John 9:4

Lois Snell

Spoken To About Amber, II

Chapter 18

Like most mothers, I can't begin to count the number of prayers I've offered for my children. My prayers began during pregnancy and have never ceased. I prayed long and often for Amber in particular as there was an uneasy feeling that she wouldn't live long. Amber was full of questions and wanted to experience life to the fullest. Once, she'd come running to me and asked, "Mama, when Twyla is fifteen, how old will I be?"

I tried to answer ten but a sudden chill came over me. I just stared at her remembering another such incident. In that case, we were having Thanksgiving dinner at Charlene's. Ray's grandmother, two great-aunts and I were seated at the table just as dinner was being served. Aunt 'T' said, "Oh, this is so nice, all of us having dinner together."

When she spoke those words, a sudden chill came over me. Somehow, I knew this was the last Thanksgiving dinner we'd share. One by one, I studied the beautifully aged women and sorrow filled my heart. I couldn't help but wonder who it would be, knowing it could be me. The latter part of January, Aunt 'T' was admitted into the hospital with pneumonia. She died in less than two weeks.

"Mama!" Amber snatched me back into reality. "How old will I be?"

"Ten," I whispered, my heart sinking. I couldn't look at her; I couldn't talk to her now with my heart and mind in turmoil. I went into another room as she skipped down the hallway to find Twyla.

"Oh God, please. Please."

From that moment on, I was even more prayerful for Amber. I offered prayers at all times--driving down the street, taking a silent break from my job, doing housework or cooking. Even at family gatherings, I'd go into the closet of my mind and pray. Sometimes in the middle of the night, I'd wake up and fall to my knees in prayer. Those prayers worked mighty miracles. Regardless as to my job situation, my daughters and I were never displaced. We kept a bounty of food for our table. We always had enough of everything to share with others. Unless I had medical coverage, no one in my family was ever sick, no one needed to be rushed to the hospital, nor required medical treatment in any fashion. Prayer was my secret weapon that warded off many evils, diseases and injuries. I was thankful to God for showering us with blessings, those large and those small. I still am.

One night, I woke up and began to pray for Amber. She was approximately six years old at the time. I asked God to please grant her a long life and to remove the fear of death from my heart. Even as I was praying, God spoke to me.

"She will have to fight the devil," God said.

I took this as a reprieve, feeling certain He'd just granted her a longer life span. Sudden gratitude gave way to another realm of despair--the conditions connected with the reprieve.

"Oh no, God! She's just a baby. She's too young to fight the devil," I cried.

"She will have to fight the devil," God reinforced.

"Why? What is it you want her to do?" I asked, crying and babbling.

"That is not for you to know," God said.

"But, God, she's my baby. Please, I don't want her to fight the devil. That's dangerous! Too dangerous! What if she's not strong enough? Please, please, God, can I do it?"

"No. This is for Amber to do."

"But, God--" I started.

"You cannot fight her battles, Lois," God stated. "But, you can prepare her for them."

God stated that Amber had a mission in life that potentially had the power to change the world. He entrusted her with this potential but she would have to unlock it. I begged Him to give me more information. I tried to reason with Him that I could better help my daughter if I knew what her mission was and when she'd need to perform it. God would not divulge any further details about the future. Yet, in my spirit, I knew He would equip Amber with what she needed to be the victor.

That knowledge didn't quiet the trembling in my stomach. I knew the Scripture that all things work together for the good of them that love the Lord who are the called according to His purpose. (See Romans 8:28.) This sounded very much like Amber was in the group of "the called", a chosen one. To fight the devil carried many implications with it. There are large devils as well as small ones. Let me clarify this, every devil is large. But, some devilish things can be as small as my habit of drinking too many carbonated beverages. God had spoken to me before on behalf of Amber. I knew his plan for her life was not small scale. Being human and in my limited mortal imagination, I could not even be trusted with the knowledge of what was to come.

"Before I formed thee in the belly
I knew thee; and before thou
cameth forth out of the womb
I sanctified thee, and ordained
thee a prophet unto the nations."
Jeremiah 1:5

"Thou hast beset me behind and before,
and laid thine hand upon me.
Such knowledge is too
wonderful for me; it is high,
I cannot attain unto it."
Psalm 139:5-6

First Testimony

Chapter 19

There was a critical spirit that lay within my being. Not recognizing it as such, I only knew it irritated me for people to come down front during church services and ask for special prayer for the same problem week after week. I felt they should pray for themselves and stop bothering the church with all their mundane problems. Everyone had problems, that was life. I felt if they were praying for themselves, they'd be better able to cope when problems arose. I remember the time when a member shared that he was praying for a washer and dryer for his wife. He said, "I'm putting that on God." That embarrassed me. On that day, I'd hoped there were no visitors at church to witness this and wondered what their thoughts of us, as a church body, would be if we were incapable of making simple business deals. Likewise, there were people choosing to give seemingly meaningless testimonies. The thought that they were trying to draw attention to themselves always seemed to hover in the background of my mind. I'd prided myself for not voicing my opinions about these matters. Watching the actions in quiet restraint, I felt as though I was doing no wrong. All the time, I was deceiving myself. In God's eyes, evil feelings harbored in the heart are just as vile as those committed in the flesh. I learned that from Sarah, Abraham's wife. Months, possibly years, passed with my silent judgments waging inner war.

In later years, I would learn that there are countless people who do not know how to pray for themselves. If they want deliverance from their situations, they tend to ask people they feel can get a prayer through. I've asked for forgiveness for hoping that visitors were not present the day of the incident of the washer and dryer. Had my heart been grounded spiritually, I would've been more interested in the visitors' souls being saved rather than feeling embarrassed by a testimony.

Also, I would come to learn that every testimony is not meant for every ear. Therefore, no testimony is meaningless. For the ear God intended to hear, the testimony would have a profound effect on that person's life. With what I felt was mundane, another had burdens lifted or was given crucial insight to the road that lay ahead. I thank God for allowing me to live and come into these realizations. I thank Him for opening my eyes and allowing me evaluate myself rather than nursing resentment against others.

During the time I was silently sinning in thought, God laid it on my heart to give my own testimony. I rejected it. Week after week, my daughters and I sat in the balcony and I refused the urge to come forward. I felt I didn't need to share anything of my personal life with my church family. It was boring, it delayed dismissal and it would serve no purpose. But, one sermon spoke to my heart and I couldn't remain seated. It was like a fountain rising up inside me that I knew would overflow if I didn't release it. Still, I was not willing.

Because I couldn't stop myself, I told my daughters to be still and advised them that I had to go downstairs and give my testimony. Their eyes held huge questions but their lips remained sealed.

Mindlessly, I began walking downstairs. It was not an option to turn back but I was frightened. I didn't have a clue as to what my testimony was and couldn't even imagine what I'd say. There'd been so many times God had come to my rescue. Jesus, Himself, had manifested in my presence. Jesus didn't send Rafael, nor Gabriel nor any other of the Angelic host, He'd come himself when I greatly needed comforting. I knew I was a child of the Most High God and I enjoyed being in his courts. I had many wonderful and marvelous things in which to be thankful for. But, these were my experiences. I'd deemed them personal and private, only to be shared with close friends or relatives--people of my choosing. Still, I continued to move forward though I was tongue-tied and feared making a complete fool of myself.

As I battled with the decision of what to say, God typed a message across my forehead, just underneath the skin. It read, "*THE WORDS WILL COME*." I saw it as clearly as if I were reading the headlines of the newspaper.

Before long, I was seated down front with several others who had prayer requests or testimonies to share. Hundreds of eyes stared at me and I felt extremely uncomfortable. God hadn't shared with me what I should discuss and my mind was whirling at elusive fragments. Lastly, I was given the microphone. Nervous and trembling, I stood up with a blank mind. With nothing to say, I opened my mouth to speak and the Holy Spirit poured forth the message that had many sitting on edge. The congregation's eyes were fixed on me and they seemed to be eagerly anticipating the next word that came from my mouth. I, myself, did not speak. Using my body, my person, my vocal chords, the Holy Spirit intervened for me.

Among other things, the Holy Spirit shared of the degradation I'd felt for accepting help from the welfare department and God's bringing me through critical times. This is something I, myself, would never have shared with total strangers. It was not something I'd choose to share--not even with close friends or family. Whenever I'd been forced to discuss it, I'd spelled the word, w-e-l-f-a-r-e. I couldn't bring myself to say it aloud for fear that my children would overhear and for fear that speaking it would solidify it in my life. It represented my greatest sense of shame. Yet, the year and a half I'd received help from the welfare department proved to be a true growing experience. Having gone through it, I've developed a greater sense of appreciation for and understanding of depending totally on God. It is not by our power that we're able to sustain ourselves. I also learned not to classify people by their conditions, economic or otherwise. I'd constantly begged God to allow me to find employment, to show me the meaning of my joblessness, to remove this feeling of loss and uselessness from me.

God remained silent.

He was determined that I would learn how welfare mothers were treated from perfect strangers as well as from family. In the not so distant past, I'd worn the badge of pride for being sole support of my daughters and myself. I felt and acted as though I needed no one. Seeing some of the relationships others were involved in, I'd prided myself for not "putting up with that mess." I didn't recognize that these actions and thoughts were vanity until the carpet of gainful employment was snatched from underneath my feet. I'd never much cared what others thought, yet in this degraded state, their careless and cruel words cut like a jagged knife to the heart. But God is faithful to his promise. Through love, mercy and grace, He has restored everything that the locust and cankerworm have devoured. (See Joel 2:25.)

I had no control over what the Holy Spirit chose to share with the church. I was more surprised than the congregation itself when He delved so deeply into my life--into my business. No one knew of the dilemma I'd been in; I'd deliberately kept it quiet. But, the Holy Spirit shared all and I was powerless to stop Him.

I'd expected to be somewhat shunned for my candor after service. I'd expected to receive looks of disappointment and glances of belittlement. Neither occurred.

By the time this testimony was shared, I'd weathered the storm and had been gainfully employed for several months. I left that service with a light heart and a deeper appreciation for the Holy Spirit. On that day I learned that testimonies are given for two reasons, neither of which has anything to do with the person giving the testimony. The first reason is to give God the glory. The second reason is so that chosen ears may benefit from them. Praise God for His wisdom.

"But when they deliver you up,
take no thought how or what
ye shall speak: for it shall be given you
in that same hour what ye shall speak.
For it is not ye that speak,
but the Spirit of your Father
which speaketh in you."
Matthew 10:19-20

"Tomorrow, Your Heart Will Be Glad."

Chapter 20

Years later, I was dating a handsome gentleman several years older than myself. He was kind, caring and witty. His lifetime primary focus was on family and I admired that. As relationships go, we had no major problems. However, his daughter literally hated me. She'd tried everything within her power to root me out of his life. There were many times I sat in disbelief of her actions. The first irregularity I remember was an incident when we were attending a picnic at my sister's house. His daughter, then twenty-four years of age, called him at Charlene's to ask how to turn off the electric coffee pot. Another incident I found disturbing was when she called my house to advise him that Penn Square Bank was defunct. That was national news that had been airing all day. Naturally, I assumed he banked there. When I asked him about it, he had absolutely no ties to Penn Square Bank.

My job was only ten minutes away from his residence and he'd often invite me over for lunch. During the forty minutes I was there, his daughter always needed to share some news flash with him such as the neighbors next door getting a new roof as if he hadn't heard the constant loud hammering of the roofers. At this point in her life, she was still living at home and unemployed. She was a college student, a commuter--taking two classes a day. He'd baby-sit her infant daughter while she attended college. I felt that was commendable. Yet, on a daily basis, during the forty minutes I was over, she continued to leave her child for him to watch while she rested from her two classes. There were several occasions she felt she needed to share her test scores with him during my lunch hour.

In addition to her being extremely rude to me privately, always out of view of her father, there were many incidents that hinged on bazaar. The incidents kept escalating. For a long time, I accredited her dislike of me to the grieving process of losing her mother several months prior to my meeting her father. I certainly could understand that. I could even understand her being protective of her father. After all, her parents had been married some thirty plus years and he'd been out of the dating scene for at least that long. So, I didn't take it personally.

It became personal over the phone one night. I'd changed jobs and was working from two to ten in the evening. When I'd drop my daughters off at school in the mornings, I'd sometimes go visit him before I went to work. One day in particular, we both left his house when she'd returned from class. Retired military, he loved to shop on base and was going there for groceries. I had errands to run before work. Generally after work, he'd call to make sure I made it in safely or I'd call him to let him know I had. This particular night, I called and asked to speak to her father when she answered.

"Well, Lois, I just need to know one question," she said.

"Yes. What is it?"

"What happened in the bathroom?"

"What do you mean?" I asked, surprised by her question.

"Well, did you have diarrhea or something?"

"*WHAT!*"

"Well, the bathroom was all messed up and you're the only one that was over here--you know--besides Dad. And, he didn't do it."

"Girl, put your father on the phone!"

I was furious. I was nearly forty years old, had three bathrooms in my town house, and well knew how to flush the stool. While she was getting him, I wondered what type plumbing problems they were having.

When I asked him about his daughter's sewer claim, my ears burned with anger at her allegations. He shared with me his daughter's claim that I had defecated all over the bathroom and left it there. Not only that, she claimed I'd smeared it on the stool, walls, curtains and glass shower door. According to her, I'd left little snippets of toilet tissue stuck in the mire on several places of the wall. Also, she claimed I'd stomped and smeared feces into the bathroom area rugs. Those rugs were so embedded; she claimed to have washed them twice already and needed to do it again.

Even he, a loving, doting father who'd always been a faithful husband and excellent provider for his children, could not believe this outlandish vicious attack. He'd repeatedly questioned her as to why she hadn't left the evidence until he'd returned from grocery shopping. After all, they had two bathrooms. She could have easily shut the door to the main one and used the second should she have need. Her answer was that she just couldn't stand to see it that way and continued to hold fast to her smelly lies. I felt his daughter, now twenty-six, couldn't stoop any lower. Not ever. Voiced words, whether blessed or evil, often have a lasting effect.

That was the beginning of the crumble of our relationship. I know parents aren't responsible for their children's crimes and, this was a crime. I felt it was a crime committed against me. I honestly felt he should've begun to correct the problem starting with the incident of the coffee pot. But, he didn't realize there was a serious problem until she'd called pretending the house was being burglarized. Now, she hadn't dialed 911 for emergency, nor had the burglar alarm been activated to alert the officials. She'd called her father to come home immediately and protect her from dangers unseen.

She was a woman who'd succumbed to desperate measures. I kept wondering what she'd do next. I'd overheard her comment never intended for my ears that he was going to marry me and I would get all her mother's stuff. Never having worked for a living or purchased anything with money she'd actually earned, she didn't know the pride associated with being independent. She didn't realize that I didn't need her mother's stuff, much less, didn't want it. I had my own. Also, in her mind, she could not perceive that one need not sit and wait for others to die so they may have something they deemed valuable.

The night of the bathroom incident hurt me deeply. Such venom would not be given safe harbor in the mind of an ornery child. The thought of a twenty-six year old voicing such was more than I could bear. I cried that night--hot, salty tears of indignation, tears of confusion.

I tried to pray but nothing would come out. I didn't know how to ask God to fix this. Words, even thoughts eluded me when I tried to speak. Down on my knees and moaning, I lifted up heavy arms with no words.

"Go to sleep, my child. For, tomorrow--your heart will be glad," God spoke.

I crawled into bed and pulled the covers up wondering how. How could my heart possibly be glad?

Depression and grumpiness greeted me the following morning. My daughters asked what was wrong as I wasn't cheerful like usual. I told them I didn't feel well. That was no lie, I felt terrible inside. I dropped them off at school and tried to find things to do to keep me away from home. I didn't want him calling me as the sound of his voice would remind me of the unstable character of his daughter. He did manage to catch me at home shortly before I left for work. He called to apologize for her. I was in no mood to listen to second-hand apologies. For that matter, neither did I want to hear first-hand apologies.

When you're in a serious relationship, you must weigh the options. What lies ahead? Do problems outside the relationship threaten peace of mind within the relationship? Are there traits of undisclosed mental illness within this family unit? If there is, can you deal with it? Do you want to? Be real with your answers. And, be real when analyzing situations. The old adage is true, actions speak louder than words. Is this the life God's chosen for you?

I left for work early. Looking like the picture of gloom, I walked into my friend Cynthia's office. She had several employee files on her lap and was entering information onto the system. Cynthia looked up as I entered. "Whoa, what's wrong with you?"

"Nothing," I said not wanting to discuss the matter. I wanted it to disappear, to be gone, to never have happened. I hadn't come into Cynthia's office for sympathy. I needed to be around someone that I knew cared about me, someone who wasn't vile or manipulative. I wasn't seeking advice, just comfort. Plus, I knew she hadn't had the misadventure to be blatantly accused of hurling feces. She would never understand. I could get no help from the library. As far as I knew, there were no self-help manuals written on the subject.

"That's the biggest nothing I've seen in a while," Cynthia said. "Okay, Cynthia," I said while sitting down facing her. Listening, she kept working on her files. I was not offended because I knew she had she had a deadline to meet.

"I have a problem."

"What is it?" she asked.

I shared with her the details of the crime I was accused of, defacing a bathroom. Her eyes were glued to her monitor as she listened. After all the gory details were revealed, I waited for a moment for her to respond.

"Well--Lois," she started. Sudden laughter sprang up in her like an uncapped oil gusher. She tried to hold it back but couldn't. Cynthia covered her face with the files and her feet tap danced on the floor.

"Cynthia!" I shouted. My face was just as suddenly distorted with a mixture of disappointment and confusion. She was trying her best to stop laughing but couldn't. I began to laugh, too. The weights were air lifted from my heart and I laughed until I cried. My heart was glad--just as God said it would be.

Deep wounds can only be healed by God and His healing is always complete. The idea, the very idea of something as bizarre and heinous as this, was so ridiculous until it was humorous. I hadn't imagined it possible. We simply roared with laughter. Others came by, their questions always the same. "What's so funny?"

Tearing at the eyes, and shaking her hands, Cynthia responded, "You wouldn't believe it if I told you."

We finally managed to gain control of ourselves. Cynthia straightened her face up and apologized for laughing. We burst into another round, holding onto our stomachs because by now they ached.

By the time I left her office, I felt like a different person. I had a great day at work, far different than my expectations. I know that God led me to Cynthia's office in His divine will of making my heart glad. From that day to this, I've remembered this incident through different eyes. Laughter rather than anguish is associated with it. I'm thankful to God for changing an awful situation into a humorous memory. I'm thankful to Him for answering the prayer I couldn't even utter.

"Likewise the Spirit also helpeth our infirmities:
for we know not what we should pray for as we ought:
but the Spirit itself maketh intercession for us
with groanings which cannot be uttered.
And he that searcheth the hearts knoweth
what is the mind of the Spirit,
because he maketh intercession for the saints
according to the will of God."
Romans 8:26-27

In His Glory!

Chapter 21

Along with approximately five other adults, I was attending a planning session of some committee at my church. We were in the choir room adjacent to the offices behind the sanctuary. My daughters were out in the vestibule using the telephone. When the meeting was adjourned, we sat talking for a few minutes before deciding to leave. Not realizing my daughters were in the outer courts, the trustee locked the sanctuary door. When I advised him that my children were outside, he let me in to get them. Knowing he needed to leave for work shortly, I advised him that I wouldn't be long.

Stepping one foot into the sanctuary, it felt as though I were stepping onto a cloud. One foot felt the hard texture of the carpet-covered hallway floor, the other--clouds in the sky. I remember thinking how weird that was and hurriedly stepped inside. The other foot was now treated to the delightful billowy clouds. I'd always enjoyed the sense of calm my church offered me. But this was far different than usual. A peace, that could only be perfection, filtered through the air. I was the only one in the sanctuary. That is, the only natural being. I hurriedly passed the organ and drums and had reached the third row of pews. All the while, I was walking on clouds--soft and billowy. My feet were not touching the floor. I was not floating or being pushed by strong winds. I was just walking on clouds, as though it were the most natural thing to do.

"Slow down, slow down," the voice of God called. God's voice was rich and authoritative, yet warmed by love. As I slowed down to enjoy my walk, I looked for someone other than myself inside the sanctuary. What I found was--the presence of God. By this time, I was midway through the sanctuary and I witnessed God's Holy presence beaming down from the high places. There was a massive explosion of lights looming above, lights like fire, not fluorescent bulbs. The ceiling had been uncapped; it was nowhere to be seen. Indescribable beauty, God's Holy Fire, was everywhere beaming down in such splendor that I was humbled, filled with gratitude, love and appreciation all at once.

The most brilliantly orchestrated display of fireworks cannot rival the glory of God.The color spectrum was beyond my knowledge, beyond my imagination. Splendidly magnificent beaming streams came from the core, spectacular rolling clusters, and gigantic splinters of fanciful lights more colorful than the rainbow were showering down toward me. Vibrant colors danced everywhere. Rolling puffs as well as gentle splinters of smoke danced with the lights. Although they came extremely close, I felt no fear for my life or danger that I would be harmed. Glorious showers of love were directed at me. I felt the greatest warmth and love emanating from this miraculously brilliant concentrated energy. Although the fiery display continually danced above, the warmth was not heat like fire that we know: It was the warmth of total love, pure, un-pretentious love. I was in God's presence like never before.

I'd never doubted God's existence. Raised in a loving Christian home, baptized at the age of twelve, and taught to read the bible, I had a good upbringing. Mama and Daddy offered us the very best they had. But, by far, the most precious gift they could've given us is the introduction to God and Jesus early in life. They did this without fail, without thought and without pretense. They were not preachers of God's Holy Word, but they lived their lives according to God's Word and we were the better for it. As I marveled in the beauty of God's Holy Fire, I knew with certainty my upbringing had not been by chance. God had ordered it. He'd deliberately placed me in a home He trusted to mold me to the point that I could be placed in His presence and ask what He required of me. Not only to ask this question, but to follow through with His instructions.

I knew I needed to gather my children so we could leave as the trustee was waiting for us. All my senses were alive, keener than ever before. But, being witness to the glory of God was too powerful and too beautiful a moment to toss aside. I wanted to prolong the moment, to savor it. I wanted to absorb being in the presence of God and commit it to memory. Then, I'd be better able to share the experience with my children and others. Still, walking somewhat with more vigor than I'd choose to, I basked in the glory of God. I've heard the term 'raising the roof' before, but God literally, physically raised the roof of the sanctuary. It could not be seen for the vastness of His glory. I actually saw His glory, felt the warmth and radiance of His holy presence. The sanctuary was filled with His holiness. Everything about Him is pure, all-consuming and righteous. There was, there is absolutely no negativity in Him.

Everything there was sacred--everything, including me. At that moment, I felt spotless, blameless, as though the blood of Jesus had freshly washed me clean. I felt loved, and wonderful, and beautiful. A wellness of spirit never before known came over me. Without doubt, without hesitation, I knew that God is real.

While wondering how I could feel wellness of spirit rather than being deeply disturbed by being in the presence of God, the knowledge dropped into my spirit. God was not calling me to the finality of sleep. He had not come to judge my past at this time. I was His child and His pupil. One, like you, He greatly loves. As God stands in yesterday, today and tomorrow, He viewed me as the finished product once He'd put away his pruning shears. Therefore, His love and approval of me could only be accepted into my soul as wellness of the spirit. Praise God for His long suffering!

I regretted reaching the door. When my feet stopped moving, I began to look around the sanctuary. With the exception of the ceiling, everything was still intact. The glory of God continued to be descending from it, bouncing all over the place at once. It was so spectacular, so un-imaginable. This is impossible in the physical world, but it's a simple matter for God, the Creator of all good things. Any place, familiar or unfamiliar, can become holy when God says so. I knew He wanted to talk to me. My only explanation for knowing this is that God placed the knowledge in my spirit.

"Okay, God. What is it you want with me?" I asked while looking around at the various places in which I could serve. Now, these words may seem cold and indifferent, but truly they were not. They were asked with a humble heart, a spirit ready to receive instruction with no pretense regarding my character. Certainly, He had instructions for me in the area of service. To show up, in His glory, He surely had work for me to do.

"I'm already teaching Sunday school. I may not be good at it, but I'm trying. I sing in the choir. I can't sing, but I'm trying."

These were areas in which I felt inadequate, but God's love blinded my own inadequacy. I felt no conviction of spirit for not teaching perfectly or singing perfectly while I was in His presence. I suppose He was content with my trying. He had the power to change my vocal chords or enlighten me with new and innovative teaching strategies; but, God did not comment or give me direction. He listened quietly as I continued guessing what He wanted. I looked to where the ushers stood.

"God, you know I don't like to be on my feet for any length of time. It bothers me," I said remembering the spur that was trying to grow on my heel and how I had to mentally will myself to stand still. I was amazed at the level of comfort I felt with Him, but I knew even then, it was only because He permitted it. He didn't need me extremely afraid or over anxious at this time. That wouldn't best serve His purpose. Then, I looked to the pulpit.

"Now God, You know that's not me," I said earnestly and with respect.

"No, it's not," My God spoke at last.

Even though He had not spoken thus far, I didn't feel as though I was involved in a one-way conversation. There was acknowledgement in the spirit realm. Being in His presence was conversation. His presence conveyed His love for me without a single word. God's presence conveyed His protection. His presence conveyed that I was important to Him. By allowing me to glimpse His Holy Fire, God conveyed there was a purpose for my life. This is conversation, marvelous conversation.

"But, Lois," God continued. "Your writing is you. Your writing is a gift. It's a gift I bestow on you. It's to be used for my edification."

"Yes," I nodded in awe.

He knew my name! He knew my talents. It always shocked me anew whenever God identified me by my name or commented on my innermost thoughts. I already knew in my heart that my ability to write was a gift from Him. Friends and family members had voiced these same sentiments. But I was surprised to hear God state it. I was surprised beyond measure to learn that it was to be specifically used for His edification. I mean, how could I edify God? *HE' S GOD!*

I'd been writing little worldly manuscripts that I hadn't accredited as being worldly. I'd carefully defended them as life, tastefully written. God would have one hot or cold, not lukewarm. A child of his should not be writing world pleasing manuscripts. Suddenly, I realized why my works hadn't sold. I'd received many complimentary rejections praising my work, praising my ideas and efforts. But, they were all rejections, rejections because I was writing to please the world in which I lived rather than my God who'd granted me life, my God who'd sent His son, Jesus, to the cross for my sins.

You just know when your conversation with God is over, or rather, His conversation with you. He's straight forward and to the point, never wasting idle chatter. God imparts the wisdom He's willing to share with you at the time. He then allows you the choice of making the right decision with it. It's important to know that you still have the option to make the wrong decision. He will not force His will on you, you must choose it.

I stood in His glory a moment or so longer. I wanted to soak up the energy, to feel the radiant blessings of His love in present time. I wanted my eyes to continue to enjoy the fiery display, my heart to continue to feel the peace, my mind to completely comprehend perfection. Even standing in His presence, I couldn't fully comprehend it. I could only understand and identify with the facets of God's character He was willing to impart with me. The main point I understood was God's love--love in its most pure form. God had given me my commission. There was nothing more that needed to be said.

When I knew He was through sharing, I opened the door, stepped outside and told my daughters it was time to leave. They needed a moment or two to gather their belongings and to put the telephone away. When we stepped back inside the sanctuary, I was saddened that the glory of God was no longer visible. Not only was it no longer visible, but there was absolutely no evidence supporting that it had ever been present. The ceiling was restored to its original, now simple, grandeur with height limitations. How sad.

I definitely wanted my daughters to experience the love and beauty of God's presence. I wanted them to be able to walk on clouds, to view perfection. I wanted them to taste of the love that cannot be sampled through human taste buds. I wanted Twyla and Amber to feel the Holy fire that burns clear down to the soul but does not harm the flesh.

Reviewing my precious moments in His glory, I walked realizing how hard the sanctuary carpeting felt underneath my feet. Until now it'd been plush, far more so than that in the outer courts. I longed to walk on clouds again. In my mind, I continued to feel God's love and protection, His forgiveness and tender mercies.

Absolutely no love on earth can compare to the love of God, not even the love of one's mother or child. God's love is all encompassing, to every fiber of your being. God's love loves you in spite of your flaws. It's even far greater than the love you feel for yourself. His love is unconditional. It is not tossed by the wiles of the wind, being blown in different directions at the same time. It's strong and sturdy and sure--everlasting.

God loved me even when I loved living in exact contrast of His perfect will. He loved me when I knew I was living in sin and chose to stay there. Rather than cast me aside, He chose to forgive me even though I hadn't asked forgiveness of certain things. There were high points in my life I'd wanted to savor. Asking forgiveness of them would eliminate the immediate gratification of their memories. Later, I came to realize that if they should be bitter memories rather than sweet savors, the forgiveness of God made it such. And, I was better for it.

As I stood in the glory of God, I didn't realize it then, but this shows the power of a spiritual washing. At the point of acceptance of Jesus as Christ and Savior, God, through the blood of Jesus, cast all my sins into non-remembrance. Jesus died once to cleanse all sins man would ever commit. That cleansing is for us to accept and move forward in straightness. Neither in thought nor deed should we continue to drudge up the past. God has cleansed us for a reason. When we manage to accept our cleansing and move forward, often others want to bring our polluted past to our attention. The world is filled with broken people who either don't realize they're broken or haven't assessed their damages. In their brokenness, they lash out at others in order to bandage the pain of their own lives. It's not necessary that we become angry or frustrated with these people. They're merely walking in their level of understanding. So, be patient with them, just as God has been patient with you. Try, if possible, to raise their level of awareness without offence and without piousness. Otherwise, simply advise them that God has released you from that bondage and walk away. In due season, they'll come into the realization that only God is worthy of judgment. "What shall we say to these things? If God be for us, who can be against us?" (Romans 8:31) The Holy Scriptures clearly state that God is love. (I John 4:8). Having been witness to His glory, having conversed with Him through His glory, I whole heartedly testify that--God is love.

"Now Moses kept the flock of Jethro
his father in law, the priest of Midian:
and he led the flock to the backside of the desert,
and came to the mountain of God, even of Horeb.
And the angel of the Lord appeared unto him
in a flame of fire out of the midst of the bush:
and he looked, and, behold,
the bush burned with fire,
and the bush was not consumed."
Exodus 3:1-2

"In the year King Uzziah died
I saw also the Lord
sitting upon a throne,
high and lifted up,
and his train filled the temple."
Isaiah 6:1

Soldier Standing Guard

Chapter 22

We'd moved into a wonderful old home built in nineteen hundred and twenty-nine. It belonged to Ray's grandmother. She'd become unable to care for herself and had moved in with them six months prior. Our move there served two purposes. My rent there would only be half the amount I was paying for the town house. He'd feel at ease that the home in which he was reared was not sitting idle with his grandmother's possessions locked inside.

It took me three to four months to become organized because I had to deal with two complete households of furniture. Mrs. Cook had never officially moved out. She just moved her person to their home. I'd arrive home at approximately four in the evening and would work there until midnight. It was very difficult, mentally difficult, moving her personal belongings and furnishings into the storage house out back.

My days were long and grueling. Yet at night, I slept with a strange and uncommon peace that had eluded me for many years. My daughters, now teenagers, also spoke of the peace and rest they felt there. I'd associated the newfound peace with the fact that this house was like a family heirloom, a jewel. For twenty years or more, even before my children were born, Charlene and I had visited Mrs. Cook in her home. My daughters spent the night occasionally with or without their cousins. Many a time we'd shopped for Mrs. Cook or helped her to clean. She'd sometimes call me to do chores or run errands in order to give Charlene a break. Mrs. Cook felt comfortable doing this because she knew we loved her like family. After all, she was.

I'd intentionally gone to sleep on the living room sofa. Turning in my sleep, I awoke in the midst of the night. My eyes focused on a lone soldier standing guard from a different time era. His manner of dress told me he belonged to many generations past, possibly more than a century. He wore a long calf length coat with a wide belt around the waist. Only about eighteen inches of pants legs were shown. Also, he was adorned with worn but polished military boots, a hat with a band on it. The soldier held a rifle with a long bayonet attached to the end of the barrel. He stood by the dining room entryway, approximately six feet away from me. Alert, he stood erect with the look of determination on his face. His eyes were keen, focused like a sharpshooters ready to attack.

He realized that I saw him and turned to me, nodding in respect.

"Don't be afraid, Ma'am. I'm just here to protect," the soldier said.

I looked deeply into his eyes and knew he was telling the truth. There was no need to ask him what time period he belonged to. He was on duty now. I was not afraid. Not of him, not of the weapon he carried. I could tell the spirit of God rested within his being. I nodded acceptance, turned over and went back to sleep.

The following morning, there were no signs that there had ever been a soldier standing guard. I didn't know if his assignment was to protect my family, the grounds on which the house stood, or some other unseen entity. But, I felt protected. I felt no evil seen or unseen could come against us at that point.

"I will both lay me down
in peace, and sleep:
For thou, Lord,
only maketh me dwell
in safety."
Psalm 4:8

Lois Snell

Angels Flying Alongside My Car

Chapter 23

For several years, I'd been working as a reservations agent for a leading car rental agency. I was very happy when landing the job because their benefits were wonderful. It seemed like the place of retirement for me. The salary was decent and overtime was offered in abundance. Overtime allowed us small luxuries thus far denied such as trips, outings and beauty shop appointments. I changed the decor of my daughters' rooms at will and was able to purchase items we'd long wanted. The occasional eating out became more frequent and the restaurant choices more varied. Working overtime didn't bother me as I was accustomed to working two jobs. I appreciated it. There was no commute to a second location and its pay overcompensated for the second job. Yet, time and injury would take its toll on my body. I developed Carpal Tunnel Syndrome.

I denied the injury as long as possible, telling myself that it was impossible to develop a debilitating injury because God knew I needed to work. Sometimes we feel we are so holy that we are not bound by natural laws. I argued with my doctor that his finding was not fact, suggesting that possibly I was trying to have a light stroke and he should check for that. It's amazing how people not learned in medical science can diagnose what their disease or injury is. I believe my doctor was a God-fearing man. He listened to my concerns and suggestions without showing irritation. He assured me I was not having a stroke and told me to find another line of work as my current one was detrimental to my health and would lead to permanent injury.

Two years passed with my taking Ibuprofen 800 on a daily basis to combat the pain in my arms and hands. The pain had become constant and unrelenting. At times, it was worse than childbirth. It often woke me from sleep and in tears. Losing work due to the pain, my paychecks suffered miserably. As time passed, the pain pills no longer worked, they only gave a mild degree of relief. I was using both hands and arms to move a two-quart saucepan from one burner to the next. Our front door was solid oak and I could barely open it. When I did, I used both hands to turn the key and the force of my body to push it open. Unlocking and opening the car door posed similar problems as I had to employ both arms to slowly pull it open. Even then, I was often in tears. Combing my hair and brushing my teeth were painfully dreaded chores. Having engaged the whole of my body to help me do daily chores, my movements were becoming more and more restrictive. Aside from waking up in the mornings, I had to mentally will myself to do most things.

There was no comfort in sleep. The pain grew worse then. It seemed as though it practiced during daylight hours for the main event on a well-lit stage at night. To comfort my arms, I'd prop them on pillows. They still felt as though they were trying to tear away from my body. My hands were often swollen at least one-third their normal size and my grip was little to nothing. Reading became an almost impossible task as books regularly fell from my grasp without warning. Likewise, the telephone fell to the floor in the midst of my conversations, again without warning. Driving was extremely scary and dangerous. Knowing my hands were likely to slip off the stirring wheel at any time, I rotated them often and prayed constantly. God did not allow this to happen. My hands were virtually useless, only serving as cosmetic purposes of giving the appearance of a whole body.

After many doctors' appointments and countless sleepless, pain filled nights, I took my doctors' advice and filed for Workman's Compensation. The company nurse asked all sorts of questions. "Do you play the piano? Do you sew at home? Do you knit or cross-stitch? Do you play tennis? Do you have diabetes? Does anyone in your family have diabetes? Do you work crossword puzzles?" She was searching for anything and everything not job related to blame my injury on. Finally, she made arrangements for me to see the hand specialist.

It was approximately eight-thirty in the morning and I was driving down the freeway in route to the doctor's office. As I drove, I felt the presence of a fleet of angels flying alongside my car. Not a large fleet--more than five but less than ten. I didn't see them with my natural eye, only with my spiritual eye. There was bright sunshine beaming down on the Earth. The area where the angels were flying glistened brighter. I literally mean that, where they were flying was clear of earthly nothings and they were encased in clear glistening sparks of energy. The angels began to talk to me. They reminded me that I'd prayed many times for a way out of my current position. This was my way out, they informed me.

"Oh no, this is not my way out! I have a daughter in college and a daughter in high school. I need my job! I have to work, I have to," I said aloud and with some degree of bitterness. I knew they could come up with a better plan than that--one that I approved of.

The angels saw that, even in my extreme pain, I was still too foolish to step out on faith. They knew that my mind was confined to the natural, thereby not allowing God to work for me in the supernatural. Still tainted with the joblessness of yesteryear, my carnal mind was not prepared to accept God's divine will for my life. The angels did not exchange words with me. They did not express disappointment, disgust or anger. Neither did they return my bitter spirit. They simply flew back into the heavens taking their glistening brightness with them.

I was more than a bit angry with the angels for not staying longer to work out a better plan with me. Surely they could've brought me news that I could live with. Frankly, I didn't see anything wrong with God healing my arms. He was capable of it. He'd done it before. Jesus had raised people from the dead. He'd healed blind and lame men and reversed a twelve-year death sentence for the woman with an issue of blood. He'd cleansed lepers of their spots restoring their skin to baby-like softness. Restoring my arms and hands to usefulness would pose no problem. I didn't require a miraculous healing. Neither did I request Jesus manifest in the flesh to touch my arms with His awesome power. He could simply speak the word and it would be done. That's what I felt the angels should've come to tell me.

I knew they were headed straight back to God to report that I'd rejected His plan. Either that or they had other souls to deliver messages to. Perhaps, they would listen.

The doctor's visit went better than I'd expected. Strangely enough, he was the company doctor. I'd originally rejected him preferring to meet with someone that would have my best interest at heart. When I'd met with the specialist referred to me by my friend, Susan Richardson, he'd brushed my injury aside. He asked if I had a lawyer. When I'd answered yes, he told me he was certain I'd made many friends at work and he knew I didn't want to "mess that up." He literally told me to take a pain pill and left the room. I didn't know the exam was over until the nurse entered and advised me. I was hurt and confused. I called him later and expressed my opinion of his lack of interest in his patients. Surprised by my call and the anger in my voice, he agreed that he had rushed the exam (There was no exam, just advice from a doctor by degree, not by heart.) and asked me to make another appointment. I was determined that he was not to receive one red cent from me and I discouraged anyone I saw with an ace bandage on their wrist from going to him.

The company specialist listened to my concerns. He did actual exams with strength and grip tests. He asked many questions and requested several X-rays of my hands and arms. He wanted to make certain there were no hairline fractures that could be causing my pain. He'd already requested and studied my medical charts from my family doctor and agreed with my doctor's findings, that I had Carpal Tunnel Syndrome. I was set up for a MRI (nerve conduction test) one month away. The company nurse had earlier commented that this would be a long, drawn out process. I was in dire need of help and didn't see it possible to wait another month for relief. Knowing the degree of my pain, I couldn't understand his allowing me to continue to work.

Less than a week had passed when I pulled into the parking lot for another day of what had become very grueling work. To my surprise, I couldn't get out of the car. I sat there, mentally willing myself to open the door but could not. I was immobilized with fear and didn't understand why as I'd faithfully come to this same job for ten years. Without warning, loud uncontrollable moans tore from my throat and fat tears rolled down my cheeks. My mind was constantly at war with by body, trying to force it to obey and go in. My body rejected my mind as though it were a foreign organ. How could this be? Your body is supposed to obey the commands sent from the brain. I knew I was sending the right signals. Why wasn't my body responding?

Others were coming in to work. They saw me, a mid-forties mature woman, crying like a baby and I didn't even care. For the first time in many years, my concern was only for myself. Reasoning was beginning to set in. I was on the verge of a nervous breakdown. I couldn't afford that right now. I still had my children to support, I still had responsibilities. The tears and cries kept coming.

The sight of the building and the huge parking lot was closing in on me. It was making me sick, physically sick. I knew that I needed to go in but I also knew it would add to the pain should I do so. I was angry because the company doctor hadn't taken me off work immediately. He knew what poor condition I was in. Then, he was the company doctor. This is what the nurse meant by it being a long, drawn out process. Their plan was to wait me out in hopes that I'd resign. I needed my job. I needed to go in. There were calls I needed to take. I needed to help ease the load of the department by being present when scheduled. My mind knew this; it kept sending the right signals to my body. The one thing I needed right now was to go in--but I couldn't. Physically, I could not.

I remembered the angels flying alongside my car. I remembered their message from God. Louder wails tore from within as I realized with greater clarity that He'd sent a message of hope and I'd rejected it. Then, He'd sent destruction: Destruction of the glue that held me together, my ability to cope. Twenty minutes after pulling into the parking lot, I drove away. Dealing with the physical pain for more than two years proved more than I could handle. Fear of termination kept me silent. The mental anguish of my futures' uncertainty weighed heavily upon my heart. I'd played the juggling act with these components and they were all crashing down on me at once.

Unfortunately, my doctor's office wasn't open that early. Needing immediate help, I drove to my sister Perlean's home. There is a sense of calmness and peace about Perl that is very welcoming. She invited me in and we headed for the kitchen where she prepared her famous iced tea. As she worked, I grabbed a dry, brown spotted plant, watered it and began pruning the dead areas away. Since I couldn't restore life to my body, at least I could revive this plant. Perl comforted me by serving a nice breakfast with tea and listening. Sisters are irreplaceable.

My doctor quickly recognized I was on the verge of a nervous breakdown and took me off work for the next several weeks. The MRI proved that my body was in dire need of repair. In addition to the injured arms, hands and fingers, I was surprised with the news that I had pinched nerves on both my elbows. The only option he, the company doctor, was able to offer was immediate surgery. Rather than fear the surgery, I welcomed it. I knew its pain couldn't be worse than the relentless pain I felt on a daily basis.

God had guided me in every situation I'd been willing to accept His guidance in. Since I desperately needed this surgery, I was certain He'd guide the surgeon's hands. I underwent the four necessary surgeries without incident. God's protection sustained me.

"Be careful for nothing;
but in everything by
Prayer and supplication
with thanksgiving
let your requests be
made known unto God."
Philippians 4:6

Lois Snell

Singing Better, Living Better

Chapter 24

The wondrous sound of gospel music invites itself into your heart, causing it to take flight without the aid of wings. It allows your soul to soar far beyond places you'd ever dare dream. Its' rhythm drums in your ears long after the chords have stopped, gospel music ministers to one's soul.

I sat in the pews of my church for many years, nodding my head, tapping my feet and allowing the lyrical expressions to wash over my soul. I listened to the words, learned the lyrics and quietly sang them within my heart. I was a good pew member. I took in the Word, took in the music, and gave what little I thought I could--not nearly my ten percent. Content with being a pew member, I'd listened to countless sermons but none had convicted me to the point of moving. None had convicted me to the point of giving my ten percent. Feeling the need to be convicted to move forward in God's Kingdom should signal there is a problem. Yes, I missed the signals. Even though I was not learned in the Biblical Word, I felt I was an alright Christian. We bend what few Scriptures we know in order to accommodate our lifestyles or level of understanding.

God began to challenge my thinking and I became interested in giving back to the church I loved so much. After careful thought, I'd joined the choir because it was the ministry I loved best. There was only one slight problem--I couldn't sing. I wasn't aware of this until after having joined the choir and since it wasn't my intent to become a star, it didn't trouble me. I only wanted to blend into the background giving support to those voices I'd long admired. Prior to then, I didn't know that one sang from one's diaphragm rather than from one's throat. Unable to distinguish one key from the next, I was happy hollering while others were singing. Yes, I thought I was singing, too.

After realizing my problem was serious, I purposely sat beside strong voices such as the wonderfully talented and hilariously funny Mrs. Louise Torrance and my friend, Charlene Smith. They'd discreetly nudge me when I was off key, which was most of the time.

I'm still grateful for their help and the sweet, genteel spirit of Mrs. Mertella Moon. It was a special treat to sit beside the beloved Mrs. Myrtle Winn whose wisdom and humor I adored. Having always loved gospel music and our choir, I wanted to remain a part of it. Our musician was extremely gifted and several of our soloists could've pursued careers as recording artists. Sometimes in my prayers, I'd ask God to help me to blend in since I wanted to promote His words, not hinder them. Yet, five years rolled by with my happy hollering and loving every moment of it.

I openly admit that I'm an addict, an addict to soft drinks. The luscious dark colas seemed to beckon my senses night or day. They were my coffee at breakfast and stimulants that kept me moving throughout the day. There were more than a few nights I sought the comfort of a quick nightcap before bed and it gave me great joy to find them on sale at the grocery store. At work, my desk felt naked without a can of pop. Although the dark colas were my favorites, I never practiced discrimination against the clears or flavors. They all were delicious and deserved a spot in my refrigerator. I simply enjoyed their taste never thinking of their syrupy sweetness or high acid content.

"Lois, you could sing better if you'd quit drinking so much pop," God spoke one evening as I headed for choir practice.

Some people call them colas, some sodas or soda pops. I call them pops. When God speaks to you, He speaks on your level: So, He called it pop. I knew I drank too much and was happy that He addressed the problem. My friends and co-workers warned me to curtail this destructive habit. However, I took notice when God warned me though I didn't quit altogether. My daily habit dropped from five or six cans to one or none. I finally got down to about three cans a week and held that for a long time. In doing so, much of my bloating disappeared. In addition, I had more energy than I'd had in a long time. I was singing better, living better. After a few months, I increased my intake to one or two a day. Having just finished cleaning the kitchen, I sat at the dining room table wondering which project I should do next. A crystal glass of clear water materialized before me on the beautiful mahogany table. Or, at least, I thought it was water. As I sat watching, it began to bubble. It bubbled up and over the rim spilling onto the beautiful table. Knowledge dropped into my spirit of what God was saying. He'd spoken directly to me before about my intake of too many soft drinks. Audibly, He'd given me the option of stopping for the love of singing for Him in the choir. I'd heeded that message, but like a chronic alcoholic, I was allowing the habit to return. Now, God was clarifying the matter by showing me what the acid was doing inside my body. This vision had a very sobering effect on me.

Hindsight is always better than foresight, it's twenty-twenty. In later years, I'd develop diabetes. Reportedly, this disease affects twenty million plus Americans. These are only the known cases. Most people have diabetes for a number of years prior to its being diagnosed. Only after having been diagnosed, I learned that other family members had battled or were battling the disease. Heredity along with high blood pressure and obesity are key factors in determining at-risk individuals. I feel certain that my over indulgence in soft drinks greatly contributed to this condition. Their liquid sugars are quickly distributed throughout the bloodstream. In addition, I loved beans, rice, potatoes and pasta dishes.

These foods are starches and turn into sugar in your bloodstream. I'd never known this before.

God certainly does not care that we have a soft drink or two. But, when soft drinks become your living water, they become your god and God does not share the spotlight with anyone or anything. He allowed the products to be formulated, produced and mass distributed. But, God never intended soft drinks to replace nature's juice in our lives. Water is God's drink of choice. Like manna in the days of old, it falls freely from the heavens. Everything should be done for the glorification of God. Simple things, eating and drinking, can become sinful if you over indulge in them. And, sin is the father of death.

NOTE:
Don't wait for a sermon
to drive you to do what
God has called you to do.

"Whether therefore ye eat,
or drink, or whatsoever ye do,
do all to the glory of God."
1 Corinthians 10:31

"Get Up And Go!"

Chapter 25

In prior years, I'd been surprised by the call from the Sunday school superintendent asking me to become a Sunday school teacher. Not the least bit interested in the ministry, I felt he could certainly find more qualified candidates than myself. Knowing I'd not studied God's Holy Word, there was no interest in attempting to teach what I didn't know. I frankly stated that to him but he advised me that training was available for teachers. Also, he commented that they preferred workers willing to be trained to those who felt they knew too much to be taught. I only agreed to join the ministry because I knew they needed the help. There were two other workers assigned to my class and we worked well as a team. He was knowledgeable in the Word and as faithful as the mailman. Rain, sleet or snow, he was there. She brought the lesson to life for our young pupils. I brought the creative energy into the class. We enjoyed the informative Bible study on Wednesday nights. Therefore, we did a great job of teaching. Our Bible study was always followed by a spirited heartfelt prayer meeting where old time hymns and spirituals separated the prayers being offered. It was very inspiring, motivating and uplifting. Wonderful. It was wonderful. Just being there blessed my soul.

Although I enjoyed teaching the class, it was not a burning desire of my soul. It seemed almost anything could pull me away or cause me to be late. I read the Scriptures, explained in detail what had been explained to me. But, I hadn't prayed to God for understanding of His Holy Word and didn't know I had the responsibility to do so. The only time I felt a passion for the work was when I was actually doing it. Mama taught me to do whatever I did to the best of my ability. I knew I was faltering here. I loved the children, loved working with them and they loved and respected me. I knew I was harming them by not being there consistently. I wasn't teaching them by example what I'd want them to learn, obedience to God.

One Sunday morning, I was contemplating not going. It didn't matter, I told myself. Deacon McCullough would be there, he always was. He was well able to teach the class without my help. Ten minutes before Sunday school started, I was still lying in bed--thinking, feeling guilty. I debated quitting the assignment because I couldn't seem to make myself become dedicated. Having become thirsty for the Word, it was not an option to quit the Wednesday night classes. I began to pray.

"God, please hear me. I don't know what to do about Sunday school. I enjoy it when I'm there but I just don't have the dedication I need to continue. I don't know if I'm doing a good job, if I'm teaching the right way. I feel that You want me there. I know I'm good for the children. But, I'm not committed--please, give me the dedication I need---"

"Get up and go!" God spoke while I was in the midst of my prayer. His voice was tinged with annoyance. This is another of the few times God interrupted me in the midst of my prayer. His statement confirmed that He is ever listening, ever wanting to be in communion with His people. Don't think your prayers are empty utterances. God does hear them and will answer in His time.

You've heard it said that we're often our own biggest critics. This is true. We spend many hours in harsh judgment of our own actions. We're so consumed with the failure we see that we fail to see the good fruits of our labor. Now, that attention to failure is not sent of God. It's the evil ones' ploy to keep you walking in condemnation, in disobedience which will lead to ultimate failure. Don't think I'm saying that God will accept mediocre work. He does not. Remember the Scripture that He'll have you hot or cold, or spew you from his mouth? (See Revelation 3:15.) If you're walking against God's perfect will, acknowledge that fact. Sincerely ask for forgiveness then walk in the straightness the blood of Jesus allows you. Don't try to solve your problems using your own power. It takes the power of God to make the transition complete. By all means, accept and love God's correction.

"My son, despise not
the chastening of the Lord;
Neither be weary of his correction:
For whom the Lord loveth
he correcteth."
Proverbs 3: 11-12

Forgiveness For Having My Children Out Of Wedlock

Chapter 26

Aside from God, my children have always been my greatest source of inspiration. From the time they were born, they were the embodiment of love, beauty, happiness and joy. I'm not one who believes young ladies should parade themselves in front of the church to ask for forgiveness for making a mistake. I never felt my children were mistakes. They were not planned, but they were not mistakes. Every child God allows to be conceived has a purpose in this world. Every child conceived is planned by God. Besides, I wasn't about to distort, discredit, dishonor nor delude what gave me joy, love and determination. Neither in thought nor deed should God's gift of love be tarnished.

My daughters knew they were loved. They had no reservations about being a product of a single mother. They realized that quality relationships had little or nothing to do with having two parents underneath the same roof. Quality relationships are defined with the one-on-one contact either parent has with the child. I'm not denying that I would've preferred to have been married and raised my children underneath the blessing and protection of that covenant. But, regardless to the reasons, that was not the road I'd taken and a child is not a choice you can re-think. That's how innocent lives are lost. This is something mothers-in-waiting should realize. Abortion should never be an option. It's not an effective means of birth control. If God blessed the seed, He'll bless the life. He'll provide for His child even if you cannot. God is pro-life.

The love in our home was genuine and could not be duplicated. Therefore, my daughters never allowed statistics to define them. They'd grown into lovely young women. At age twenty-one, Twyla was a junior in college and engaged to be married. Happier than I'd been in years, we all worked hard preparing for the wedding. This was a very joyous time in our lives and when any memorable event approaches, it gives way to reflections of the past. All their lives, I'd done my best to instill a sense of wholeness and oneness within my daughters, a sense of pride. I was always open and honest with them, never denying mistakes I'd made in hopes that they'd avoid them.

Something of old was tugging at my heart. I'd never asked anything of anyone for my children. Though I'd never felt I owed anyone an apology for having them out of wedlock, it dawned on me that I owed God one. Twenty-one years later, I came to this realization. It played in my mind like a silent record for a while, then burst into musical chords--loud and strong.

It was after eleven before I sought the comfort of sleep. It eluded me and I stared into the darkness. It was time, past time that I should ask God for forgiveness for having my children out of wedlock. The knowledge dropped into my spirit like a warm glass of milk poured into an empty stomach. My eyes watered from remembrances of the countless times He'd come to my aid. In my life alone, God had been my source of comfort, a provider and healer, and a father to the fatherless. God had been good to me, better than I'd been to myself. I had much to be thankful for. He'd kept me sane in an insane world. Like fresh dewdrops before the break of day, tears of gratitude trickled from my eyes.

I began to speak to God, to ask for forgiveness. As I did so, a well-lit open door appeared in the darkness, marvelous light shone from the other side. Taking note of the door that didn't belong on this wall in my room; I kept talking, thanking God for the many hurdles He'd seen us through. As I began to touch on my main point of concern, the door began to close.

He's closing the door on me, I thought while being panic-stricken. But, I was in too deep to stop now. I just kept talking, trying my best to spit out the words before the door closed and I was forever locked outside His mercy. I knew it'd been a long time in coming and I didn't fault God for turning His back on me. Regardless to what happened afterwards; I desperately wanted Him to know that I was indeed sorry for not living by His principles. I needed to let Him know.

As soon as I'd uttered the words, "Father, forgive me for having my children out of wedlock." the door slammed shut then disappeared. At that very moment, a tremendous amount of love and tender mercies encased my body like a warm blanket falling on a shivering child in the cold of night. To my surprise, I realized that the closing door was not locking me outside the grace of God. Rather, it locked my past from my future. It was as though God was saying: You're forgiven, my child. I will remember your sins no more.

This is proof that God knows our thoughts and hears our concerns even before we present them to Him. It is further proof that He, alone, is God and worthy of final judgment. It demonstrates God's long-suffering and tender mercies. Long suffering means to suffer abuse for extended lengths of time. God had waited twenty-one years for my apology and had forgiven me long before I'd asked. His hand of provision had never ceased to be present during those twenty-one years as He'd waited. But, my asking was essential and necessary. It was a key factor in my being able to forgive myself and live better tomorrows. I needed to ask for forgiveness and to know that God had forgiven me.

Women of strength seldom feel the need to apologize for much of anything. It's not that we feel we're above it. We simply don't feel that we've offended. We try our best to live our lives not hindering others and rarely see that we've hindered ourselves in growth of the spirit.

"I acknowledged my sin
unto thee, and mine iniquity
have I not hid.
I said, I will confess
my transgressions unto the Lord;
and thou forgaveth
the iniquity of my sin. Selah."
Psalms 32:5

"And it shall come to pass,
that before they call,
I will answer;
And while they are
yet speaking,
I will hear."
Isaiah 65:24

Lois Snell

Dying In My Sleep

Chapter 27

As the wedding neared, I was extremely busy, going to bed tired yet, God allowed me to awake daily with the freshness of spring. Along with my regular chores, I was totally immersed in preparations for Twyla's wedding. So immersed, I'd neglected myself though I felt fine, happy, and full of energy. Years prior, along with serious weight gain, I'd developed hypertension (high blood pressure) and was on daily medication to treat the condition. I awoke at four o'clock in the morning with a pounding headache. It seemed as though all the blood in my body was sprinting for the gold and my head was the finish line. I knew I was dying.

"Oh Lord, I don't want Amber to wake up in the morning and find me dead," I prayed silently.

I was more concerned about the devastation it would have on her than the pounding in my head. Twyla was forty-five minutes away in college and Amber would have to first deal with this alone. Memory flooded my mind that I hadn't taken my medication in two, three, four days. I was so busy with preparations; it had totally slipped my mind. I'd not been sick, light-headed or weak when I'd fallen asleep and my body hadn't warned me that there was a problem.

With the care and ease of a tightrope walker, I managed to get out of bed. The pounding in my head seemed and felt louder and harder as the blood kept racing. Now, I've been told by medical experts that one can't feel his blood racing. However, that's exactly what I felt. I slowly walked into the bathroom and opened the medicine cabinet. Each step, each movement was a major effort. I poured one tiny pill into my hand and gulped it down with water; then breathed a sigh of relief when the pounding began to slow and I could no longer feel the rushing of my blood. I was thankful to God for waking me and for giving me the knowledge not to make up for the four missed doses. Certain death would've resulted from that. Furthermore, an autopsy would've proven I'd overdosed and my children would have life-long unanswered questions and unwarranted concerns.

After checking on Amber, I eased back into my bedroom and perched on the edge of the bed for a moment or so. In what seemed like slow motion, I inched backwards into the bed resting against the headboard. After a few short minutes, knowledge that the danger had passed flooded my spirit. I didn't hear the words aloud, but I could feel God's telling me that it was okay to go back to sleep. I thanked Him again for waking me. Had I slept another five minutes, I'm not sure I would've awakened. My mind drifted to others I'd known who'd slept until death. Others who'd had high blood pressure and didn't take their prescribed medication because they, too, felt they were fine. Or, perhaps their lives had been so busy and hectic they'd also forgotten. Often times, we don't realize that whatever needs to be done will happen whether we're here to do it or not. I knew I'd been in the presence of God that night. I knew He'd once again saved me from the snares of death.

Many of us feel as though we're invincible, that we can do all things. We don't bother to add "through Christ who strengthens me" as is written in Scripture. (See Philippians 4: 13.) We set out on our mission to change the world, or at least, our corner of it. We don't credit Him for planting the knowledge in our minds of how to accomplish certain goals. We go about accomplishing and taking credit for ourselves. Moses, greatly loved by and used of God, was forbidden to enter the earthly Promised Land because he failed to give God His credit. Life is a precious gift of time with which God entrusts us to do His will. We should always be conscious of how we're spending this time as it's not our own. It's God's. With or without warning, it can be taken away within a fraction of a second. It's very important to be in daily communication with God. Please, don't ever go to bed with the sins of the day resting on your shoulders. Your tomorrow may not come.

"I will both lay me down
in peace,
and sleep:
for thou, Lord,
only maketh me
dwell in safety."
Psalm 4:8

Lois Snell

"Why Are Your Songs In The Drawer?"

Chapter 28

Writing my first song came as a surprise and new revelation. I'd written a play and needed a song to sum up my main character's life. She was dying and I wanted to show this as a "good death". Many songs entered my mind, but none captured the essence of Sabrina.

In transit to work at six-fifteen in the morning, I began to sing. Realizing the song was perfect as background music for Sabrina's death scene, I sang louder and bolder. It's a good thing no one was riding with me. Shortly before arriving, it dawned on me that the song was foreign to me. I kept searching my memory banks for its origin, thinking perhaps it was something Mama sang in my youth. Then, it became clear that it was new. This was my creation, dictated by God. He'd also dictated the scenes of the play. Primarily, they'd come in dreams. Sitting down to work, I pulled out pen and paper and began to write the song, humming and singing along as time permitted. My co-workers questioned my actions.

"God's giving me a song for the play," I said. They read the lyrics and listened closely as I tried to perfect the tune. Searching their memories for fragments of this song, all came up lacking.

From that point on, I knew when God gave me a song to write and was grateful He also gave me the melody along with the lyrics. Since I'm not musically inclined, this was an added benefit. And, the songs kept coming. I'd share them with family, friends and co-workers. I continued to write, copyright, and file them away in a drawer. Very limited in my knowledge of songwriting procedures and not ready to pursue this as career or hobby, the drawer seemed the best alternative for them. Whenever God shares something with you, it's not an option to discard it. Though I wasn't ready to pursue songwriting legalities at the time, I knew the songs had merit. Their source, subjects, and purposes were to magnify the Lord.

Some people are not inclined to go to church and make up all sorts of reasons why they don't. They're tired, it's their only day off, or they don't thrust preachers. These are simply excuses they concoct to disobey God's will for their lives. But, the spiritual yearning inside their souls won't be appeased until it's fed. They feel safe in purchasing a gospel CD and slipping it home. Gospel music has the ability to nourish wounded hearts. The songs minister to their souls and wet their appetites to become closer to Jesus and the Father. Eventually, the lyrics of the song may cause them to kneel in prayer or seek a local church home where the Word of God, through qualified ministers, can become alive in their hearts. Gospel music does not replace hearing the Word of God. Rather, it's often a precursor to it.

While attending a funeral, I became very irritated by the sermon text. The preacher of the hour and the deceased were relatives and the church was probably fuller than it'd been in quite some time. This particular preacher chose to take the opportunity to uplift himself and his children rather than God or my friends' husband. At this point in their lives, the children in bereavement were not performing up to par. They were taking the long and treacherous route far different than that taught by their parents. Yet, this preacher felt the need to boast of his children's great accomplishments during the eulogy. From the pulpit, he was literally campaigning for his son who was running for public office.

Angered by his tactics, I wanted to leave, which would've been disrespectful. How can you justify leaving a funeral before it ends? It surely would've offended my friend. Therefore, I blocked out the self-serving gloater by going into a corner of my mind. I sat there, contemplating which publishing houses I should send my manuscript to next.

"Why are your songs in the drawer?" God asked from the heavens, His voice loud and clear. It held more purpose than that of the gloating preachers'. I glanced at those sitting near me to see if they'd heard. Convinced that God's loud words were meant for my ears only, I delighted in the thought of talking to Him and was glad He'd come to take my mind off what I was being forced to hear. It's a true friend that comes to visit you when you're depressed--even if He's correcting you. Indeed, I was happy to hear from my friend--God.

"Because I'm working on Sapphire," I said mentally. "I'm trying to push my manuscript. I want it sold," I spoke loudly and clearly from my brain. Only God could hear me and I wondered why He'd asked that question when He already knew what I was doing and why.

"Lois, your songs were never meant for monetary gain. They were written for the Spirit. Why are they in the drawer?"

There He was calling me by name again. Amazingly, when God talks to you, He tells you whatever He chooses to share. You're grateful for His intervention and appreciative of His words, His wisdom. Yet, when He calls you by name, it's a sound unlike any other. You know this is not a figment of your imagination, wistful thoughts, or conjured up murmurs of what you'd like to hear. Hearing your name spoken of God has a special quality about it. It's melodious to your heart as well as your ears. You feel privileged, special and oh, so important. Plus, His coming to visit me pulled me away from my sinful thoughts. God had a twofold purpose for this conversation.

I sat back against the pew to think about it. It was true; I'd never intended to sell the songs. They were just gathering dust in my drawer, not serving their original purpose of giving God glory. He didn't speak further with me but my mind was open to new possibilities. When the funeral ended, I drove directly to St. John Missionary Baptist Church and asked to speak with Kenneth Kilgore. Mr. Kilgore is an extremely talented musician and founder of the Ambassador's Choir, which has received both national and international acclaim. The secretaries informed me that he was away on a cruise and wouldn't return for two weeks. I made an appointment to meet with him then.

My visit with Mr. Kilgore was very fruitful. He was very kind and gracious while giving me valuable insight and advice. He also had me sing my lyrics and validated that they were worthy of production. Since he didn't write or score music, Mr. Kilgore provided me with names and numbers of other talented musicians that could bring my lyrics into spiritual magnificence. I left his office filled with hope.

It was then I realized why I'd been drawn to the choir. I'd never had childhood fantasies about becoming a star. I'd never danced on a clearing in the woods or vacant stage with a pretend microphone. Nor had I bowed before imaginary audiences. I'd loved and admired Diana Ross and the Supremes as well as other musical divas of my day, but I'd never wanted to be them. Singing was never my calling but I loved the choir. After deciding it was no longer an option to be content as a pew member, our choir was the only ministry that beckoned me.

Nothing is ever wasted with God. He has given purpose to every good thing. My years in the choir did not serve to improve my singing voice. Nor did they wet my appetite to become a singer. Those years served to open my spiritual ear to write songs that lift praises to God.

"Hear counsel, and receive instruction,
That thou mayeth be wise in thy latter end."
Proverbs 19:20

Cancer, Prayers, Healing

Chapter 29

Never having been one to complain, I'd suffered in silence for four years. I was physically sick and drained of energy. Upon returning home from work, my body needed to rest in bed for at least an hour before preparing dinner. After the kitchen was cleaned, I went straight to bed. Sometimes it was as early as eight o'clock in the evening.

I'd sought medical attention on several occasions with no determination being made as to the cause of my illness. Anemic since childhood, I was instructed to take varying dosages of iron to improve my blood level. That was the problem; I had an issue with blood. Every six months, I'd gone in for a fasting blood check while the numbers kept diminishing.

After much studying of my charts and going through the process of elimination, my doctor shocked me with the news that I most likely had cancer. My daughters and I were fortunate to have this doctor because he is a kind and caring man. He listened to his patients and did not rush through exams or prematurely diagnose erroneous problems. He watched my eyes carefully, waiting for tears, anger or denial. Neither came. I knew I was sick and very much wanted an answer to my problem, a name to the force I was reckoning with. I'd never expected that answer to be cancer. The term alone is cause for great concern. Most people instantly associate the word cancer with certain death. I'd never smoked nor spent a great deal of time around smokers and I ate healthy home cooked meals. Also, I didn't consume alcoholic or wine beverages. These were my limited views of cancer causing agents. Therefore, I never felt at risk of falling prey to this deadly disease. My doctor scheduled me for a colon screening the following week.

I chose not to discuss this visit with my daughters as there was no need to alarm them. If the tests were to prove positive, I'd wait until necessary to tell them. Their happiness and well-being were my primary concerns. On Friday, I purchased the medicine needed to clear my colon and stored it in my room. It was a dry powder mix in a large gallon jar. The instructions were to add liquid and drink it Sunday evening prior to my doctor's appointment on Monday morning. Amber found the medicine and asked what was wrong. Naturally, I tried to down play its importance. However, she'd taken medical terminology in high school and knew it was serious. Amber called Twyla to discuss her concerns. Living approximately ten miles away, Twyla came over and they both questioned me.

I had to be open and honest with them. I'd always been in the past. Besides, it would cause greater concern if I failed to disclose the true nature of my illness. So, I shared the diagnosis, cautioning my daughters not to become overly concerned because even if I did have cancer, I wasn't going to die next week. Twyla and Amber carefully and tearfully listened as I explained my reasoning for this.

Amber was only two years old when her father died. At that time, I'd gone to God in prayer requesting to be able to raise, educate and see my daughters grown and secure in their own right. I wanted to be instrumental in their growth, to continue to plant the good seeds of God, Jesus, the Christ, and the Holy Spirit. It was important that they have a good foundation so I need not worry about their salvation. God promised me that He would allow this and that promise had not been fulfilled. Therefore, I knew that neither cancer nor anything else could cause this covenant to be broken. God never breaks covenants, only humans do. I knew in my heart that I would live.

Both my daughters stayed home from school that day. Twyla drove over to be with Amber before I'd returned. I'd wanted to argue that they should attend classes, but knew their minds would be in turmoil. However, I did insist that they not attend the appointment with me. In case we were to receive unfavorable news, I'd need a few moments to organize my thoughts. The last thing I'd want is for them to see distress on my face. I had no fear of death, but pain and suffering are quite different things.

When I was awakened from the test, the doctor informed me that he found no traces of cancer. He gave no lectures of what I should do. He did not suggest I change my lifestyle or my diet. There were no radiation treatments to be scheduled, no pills to take. He found nothing wrong with my blood. My daughters and I rejoiced over the outcome. That day I felt better than I had in years. The next day, I felt even better. My energy level was restored and I was my old self again. I kept waiting for the sickness to return. It never did.

Four months later, Amber and I were sitting at the dining room table talking after dinner. I said, "Amber, you know, it's the strangest thing. I haven't been sick one day since I went for that test."

"It's not so strange, Mama," she said. "I thought you knew."

"Knew what?"

"Sunday night before your test--while you were busy taking your medicine--Twyla and I prayed for you. We didn't plan this. We didn't even know the other was praying until we'd talked later on the phone. But, about seven o'clock we both knelt down and prayed. We approached God in the same manner at the same time and asked Him for the same things. Our words were almost the exact same words. As we prayed, she, in Del City, and me, at home, we both felt the hand of God upon our shoulders."

"The effectual
fervent prayer
of a righteous man
availeth much."
James 5:15-16

"It's Alright To Ask For Things For Yourself."

Chapter 30

Later that year, Twyla and her husband, Ben, accepted employment in Dallas, Texas and moved there. When school turned out for the summer, they picked Amber up for a two-week visit. I'd recently recovered from the Flu but the cold symptoms wanted to linger. I drank plenty of orange juice and took aspirins to allow relief to attend church.

Joining the others for alter call was no different than any other Sunday. The softly playing music was alluring. It requested one to open his mind and heart and in all humbleness, silently lift his requests to the Lord. The minister intervened by lifting praises and asking requests that others were secretly asking.

My children left for Dallas earlier that morning and were on the road as I stood before the alter. With closed eyes and an open heart, I asked God to see them safely home, praying for their traveling grace at this hour as well as their return trip.

"Lois, you always put others ahead of yourself," God spoke to me. "You're not well, yet you're asking for others. It's alright to ask for things for yourself."

Tears stung at my eyes, tears of joy. The voice of God was more distinct and clear than that of the minister who spoke through an expensive microphone. I clarify this at every instance because it's not normal and it always surprises me anew. It's natural and right that we, as mothers, put our children's needs before our own. God expects that of us; He gave us the heart and mind to do so. Yet, He does not want us to be so blinded by our love for our children that we neglect basic requests for ourselves. We must, at all times, remember that we, too, are His children. His love for us is even greater than our love for our children.

This is further testimony that God knows all about us. We consider the flu or a cold a minor thing as we generally have at least one or two a year. Seldom do they require medical attention, just proper rest, aspirins and plenty of liquids. Yet, God commented that I wasn't well. He knows us intimately and He cares deeply for us.

NOTE: Remember that
you, too, are God's child.

"Call unto me,
and I will answer thee,
and show thee
great and mighty things
which thou knowest not."
Jeremiah 33:3

Reprieve

Chapter 31

One month before Christmas, I was given the responsibility of chairing the Christmas program for my church. Due to prior commitments, the original Chairperson was unable to continue. Never having chaired the program before, I was honored to have the privilege. Every day after work, I'd stop by the Christian Book Store or library and read Christmas plays. When I ran across the right one, it would be like a rhema word spoken unto my soul. God would direct me. Nothing I read held any interest or was remotely appealing. I kept reading and searching yet nothing stirred my soul. Time was of the essence. It dawned on me that I would have to write the Christmas play. The knowledge lay dormant in my spirit for two days. During that time, I kept asking for direction but once again, God remained silent. We were down to three weeks before Christmas and I had not picked up the pen.

Having offered my prayers, I went to bed like so many other evenings. Later that night, I awoke gasping for air, drowning in a river of crystal blue waters. Now, this alone is a paradox as river waters are often murky and green. The person drowning in the river had a different body type than mine. We were different races; she had blonde hair and blue eyes. But, my spirit was injected into her body and I could feel what she was feeling. I saw through her eyes. As she and I struggled against the tides, I felt her desire to live. We struggled harder to overcome the merciless waters, but could not. I felt her death--her body sinking to the depth of the river. At the point of death, I felt her soul being reclaimed by God who'd granted her life in the beginning. Her body lay sprawled on the river bed, eyes glassy, and mouth gently open. Then the soul--a nearly invisible replica of her body that could be seen clear through like a crystal glass of water--lifted from her body drifting upwards, upwards through the beautiful blue waters to the bright shining light beyond. The drifting upwards was not at will, it appeared to be drifting, but I felt it being drawn with neither power nor desire to resist. Her soul could not be seen through human eyes, only through eyes of the spirit.

I was able to breathe again. I thought I'd awakened from what was a most horrible nightmare. Then, I saw her in the midst of a crowd looking for her daughter who was only four years old when the mother drowned. Again, I saw through her eyes. I felt the chilliness of her flesh as she walked among strangers in a two-piece blue suit while others were adorned in warmer clothing while shopping. She was desperately seeking her child, showing her water stained picture to perfect strangers. I felt her hearts pain as she was ignored and brushed aside by others too busy with their own lives to care. The visions continued to unfold. Time would prove that Jesus had granted her a brief reprieve. She was to guide the path of her daughter who'd grown up and chosen the profession of a call girl. She was astounded as she slowly realized that twenty years had passed since her death as it only seemed like yesterday.

At that point, I awakened and was back in my body--in my own room--in my bed. I saw through my own eyes: But, the images and life saga of this family were alive within my spirit. I sat straight up in my bed talking to God in the darkness. I was excited, alive and alight with new energies.

"Okay, God, okay! Is that what You want me to write? Is that what You want me to write?" I asked over and over again. God did not speak the words aloud to me but I knew in my spirit this was my answer. This had not been a regular dream or nightmare as I'd assumed. It had not been an ordinary vision. I'd seen many during the course of my lifetime. There was purpose with this viewing, purpose with this entanglement of lives. I'd been privy to these circumstances to be able to do justice to the mother's character with my pen.

"Okay, okay, I'll do it! I'll do it, God. But, what, what shall I call it?" I asked. REPRIEVE lit up in my mind like a light bulb. "Okay, I'll call it Reprieve. Is that alright with You?" In my spirit I knew that it was. I'm not sure how I managed to get back to sleep that night. Arriving at work the following morning, I took out my paper and pen and began to write Reprieve. I was thankful to have a job that I could do both their work as well as mine at the same time. Not losing my concentration, I wrote in between calls. At breaks and lunch, I didn't need food. The food God had poured into my soul came forth on paper and my senses never dulled.

Reprieve is not your average Christmas play. I knew I'd be treading shallow ice trying to sell this idea to the Sunday school superintendent. Yet, it was not an option to tarnish what God shared with me. He had mighty plans for this work. God was targeting someone in specific and He'd speak to their soul through this play. I neither knew nor cared for whom it was written. It could've been many people as we never know what lies in the private lives of others. He may've been speaking to devout Christians, staunch in their judgments of others. It wasn't my business to know who God was reaching out to. My business was to write what God had given me and to have it performed to the best of my ability. I wrote and proofread scene after scene giving exactness to the things I'd been privy to. My hand literally danced across the pages.

"God, you know they're not going to allow me to perform this play at church," I said aloud.

"Write the play," God spoke with authority.

"But, I'm supposed to write a Christmas play. This is about death. It's not Christmassy," I said.

"Write the play. I've given you the basics. It's up to you to add the Christmas spirit in," God said.

God was very direct and final and I was glad to hear from Him at last. Though I knew these images were coming from Him, His words were the signature I'd sought. It proved beyond reason that I was doing His will. Thus far, I'd not felt that God held Christmas in higher regard than any other day. After all, He is God--the Creator of Heaven, Earth and the Universe. He is the Creator of all things. Jesus' specific birthday is not recorded in the Bible and I knew God is no respecter of persons. I'd never imagined what tenderness He feels for the day of Christ's birth until He'd spoken to me about it. I've had communication with God ever since I can remember and know first-hand that He's short with words--to the point. The weight of His words carries tons upon tons of meaning. So, I added the Christmas spirit in.

Beautifully potted Poinsettias lined the imaginary shopping mall while shoppers were transformed into Christmas shoppers, dressed in coats and cheerful scarves, while carrying festive bags and presents. Carolers sang in the mall to both those wanting to hear and those that did not. A Christmas tree was present in the daughter's apartment and the birth of Jesus Christ was mentioned whenever possible. Reprieve was finished within a few days. I held my breath when the proposal was presented to the Superintendent. He'd rejected far less controversial issues I'd presented as skits to be performed by my Sunday school class. He took the proposal and began to read it, quietly turning page after page. I remained quiet as he read. I didn't have a defense prepared for the play, neither was I prepared to argue its merits. To my surprise, he loved it and offered to play the role of Jesus. I was totally shocked.

Then, I remembered God's words, "Write the play." God had evidently softened the Superintendent's heart to get His message across.

From that point on, everything fell in line for the play. Even given the short notice, the majority of my original character choices accepted their roles. The beautiful, graceful and demure Ms. Deborah Smith agreed to the role of the mother. Miss Kara Droke, my friend Sharon's daughter, took the role of the grown up daughter. My daughter, Amber, replaced a young actress who was away in college as the daughter's roommate. Reverend Henry Rolfe, Jr., a dear friend and associate pastor, replaced the other and became the father. Neither of these individuals had previous acting experience but marvelously brought their characters to life. My friend, Cynthia, stepped in at the eleventh hour and sang an original song written specifically for the play. Anyone that tried to throw a snare in this program was quickly put on quiet mode. God is awesome and just. He will not allow mere people He's created to disrupt a program He'd designed.

The play was performed beautifully. In one fashion or another, it touched the hearts of all who attended. Without my prying into for whom it was written, REPRIEVE accomplished the desired goal for the Almighty's purpose.

"Beloved, believe not every spirit,
but try the spirits whether they are of God:
because many false prophets
are gone out in the world.
Hereby know ye the Spirit of God:
Every spirit that confesseth that Jesus Christ
is come in the flesh is of God."
I John 4:1-2

"This Is Your New Church Home."

Chapter 32

After much convincing from both Twyla and Ben, I agreed to move to the Dallas area with them. Shortly after my wavering decision, they advised me that they were planning to have a baby. I honestly felt they were kidding, using this as a ploy to make my decision stick. It was true. I know how important the grandparent figure is in a new mother's life. There were countless days I'd wished for that luxury. I'd always promised my daughters I'd help them when they became parents. Two months after I arrived, they became proud parents of a handsome baby boy. Upon Twyla's return to work, I'd baby-sit my grandson during the day and work part time at night.

The thought of leaving my church home of thirty years had given me grave concern for weeks prior to my leaving. As the time approached, it became less difficult. When God commands something, He causes a sense of peace to come over those willing to accept it. God was using Twyla and Ben as a tool to pry me out of Oklahoma. I'd been prompted to move for years but kept waiting for events to happen. Primarily, I wanted both my daughters out of school. Amber graduated in May and we moved the first part of July. I loved my church family and was filled with emotion when saying good-bye to them. Yet, as I drove away, there was a feeling of completion in my spirit. It was as though I'd come full circle.

Certainly there would be many wonderful churches in Dallas. I'd search until I found one that was right for me. My Oklahoma friends had already given me suggestions of churches I should visit but, a church home is not something you can allow others to choose for you. It must be a very personal choice. God has not called every minister that speaks with an eloquent tongue. Some minister for personal gratification, some because they're descendants of a fine line of ministers. Some take on the role of ministering to souls for money. But, they that are the called are worlds apart. God speaks to their spirits in both visions and dreams. He chooses their paths, orders their steps and touches their hearts. God intimately converses with them, guiding them in leading His church. It is vital that I hear messages by a minister that is called by God.

My daughter and son-in-law belonged to a church that was a forty-five minute drive which included three different highways. I was accustomed to stepping from my front porch and sitting in the choir stand in less than ten minutes. Needless to say, their church did not appeal to me. They'd shared wonderful stories of personal growth and enrichment since they'd joined. Their eyes were alight with love and gratification when they spoke of Concord Missionary Baptist Church and Pastor E. K. Bailey. Knowing God is in every church, I never doubted them. But, I wanted to be closer in so I'd be available to participate in various ministries.

"Twyla, I know your church is right for you. I'm only going there to support you but I have no intentions of joining. I'll find a church in the neighborhood, one that's right for me," I said as we headed for church. This was my first time to visit their church.

"Okay, Mama. That's fine. I just want you to experience Concord," she said warmly. Ben smiled and turned his head as if he knew something I didn't. They let the matter drop and we enjoyed lively chatter during the long commute. Finally, she turned into the parking lot. The church was huge; three to five times the moderate size of my Oklahoma church home. I didn't need a further deterrent, but this certainly was one. I'd never wanted to belong to a large congregation. I liked the down home friendliness and fellowship of smaller churches and always wanted to feel God's presence where I worshipped. Though spectacular and beautiful, this was not my style. *Oh no, this will never work for me*, I thought.

"This is your new church home," God's voice rang loudly in my ears as the car was still moving. His words were very clear so that I wouldn't be able to misconstrue His meaning or doubt from whom they came. He made a statement. It was precise, not up for interpretation or discussion.

I looked around to see if anyone else heard the statement. Surely they must have. Amber, Twyla and Ben were engaged in their own conversation. Twyla had just pulled into a parking spot and stopped. They'd heard nothing. As we approached the front doors, we were greeted with out-stretched hands and genuinely warm smiles. This was my first experience attending a church that employed greeters as their frontline of worship. I was impressed, not only by the act but by their level of sincerity. Concord's twenty-fourth year anniversary was being celebrated. As usual on anniversaries, a guest minister preached the sermon. We sat upstairs in the balcony. Sometime during the service, I felt hands on my shoulders. This shouldn't be since I knew no one in the Dallas area with the exception of my children who were sitting on either side of me. I turned to see who was there and what they needed. A beautiful thirty something usher smiled and stooped down to whisper.

"It's okay. There was a wasp crawling on your back but he took care of it," she said as she pointed to the male usher beside her.

"Thank you," I said in awe to both of them. This is a shining example of the glorious protection of God. I'm allergic to wasp stings, didn't even know I'd come in contact with a wasp. Yet, there I sat among two thousand plus other souls and God directs the ushers to the wasp crawling on my back. The lyrics of one of my favorite hymns states, "His eye is on the sparrow and I know He cares for me." How much smaller is a wasp than a sparrow?

When the doors of the church were opened, I gladly accepted the call. A stranger to this city, I'd never heard my pastor preach, didn't know if he could or not. I'd not met him before and wasn't sure which of the ministers sitting on the podium was Dr. E. K. Bailey. We live in a world where so much emphasis, trust and value is placed on leaders. In this case, not only lives but eternities were at stake. Yet, I hurriedly walked down to join the Concord Church not because of the near mishap with the wasp. I came forward because I'd heard the voice of God saying, "This is your new church home."

"The steps of a good man
are ordered by the Lord:
and he delighteth in his way."
Psalm 37:23

Promises Of Blessings Sealed With A Covenant

Chapter 33

For as long as I can remember, I'd always been a giver. This generosity of the heart was a beautiful character trait of my mothers, Daddy Crooks' and Mama Elm's. Though I'd directly inherited this from both sides of my family, it was Daddy Crook and Mama Elm who'd watered it, nourished and polished it. From the tender age of three years, I'd watched and partook in their giving on a daily basis. Their actions honed this quality in year after year. Therefore, I loved to give, never expecting anything in return and never needing anything in return. My gratification, like that of my forefathers, was in the giving.

It's not unnatural that I'd want to help others that shared my plight. From that day to this, there has been tenderness in my heart for single mothers, single income families and orphans. I wanted to lift their burdens, to ease their way. When I began to write some years prior, I'd promised God that I'd greatly bless others if He allowed my works to sell. Of course, I wanted them to sell well. It was not an empty promise. It was a deep yearning within my soul. I often mapped out this desire in my mind; visiting it again and again, refining it to a point that it became a reality before time. I continued to write, sending out submission after submission and getting rejection after rejection. The rejections never bothered me much as this came with the territory. I wrote closures to my heart and openings of things I'd like to see. I wrote of the degradation of being raped. With my pen and paper, the rapist was sentenced to a life term without the possibility of parole. My pen happily placed him in a maximum security facility where men bigger and stronger than he would undoubtedly rape him. I dealt earnestly with issues of hurting spirits of people I knew, writing closures for them. I wrote positives while dealing with very negative situations. I was busy writing worldly issues when God had not called me to be a worldly writer. He'd called me to be a spiritual writer, more specifically, a

Christian writer. And, the rejections, filled with flattery, continued to roll in. It took years to sink down into my spirit that I couldn't write for both God and the world. I felt God should allow these works to sell because they were issues that seriously needed to be dealt with. It never dawned on me that He had other writers, more capable than I, that He'd called for those purposes. My manuscripts were worldly, while my poetry, songs and plays were Christian based. The poetry and plays were well received yet, the manuscripts weren't. I'd held the manuscripts in high esteem. In them, I was making right many wrongs although I'd never asked God's permission to write those manuscripts. I simply wrote the pain out of my heart and expected to be compensated for it. "Vengeance is mine; I will repay, saith the Lord." (Romans 12:19) I'd heard this Scripture all my life. But, I honestly didn't feel I was acting in vengeance since I was only putting my feelings on paper.

God wants our hearts clear. He wants our minds clear. Clear to do the good works He's chosen us to do, the works we were born to do. It appeared that God never chastised me for writing the worldly manuscripts. He allowed the words to flow from within my soul like water rushing downstream. He allowed the written words to cleanse my spirit, healing old wounds that silently cried fresh blood daily. Forgiveness has to sink well within the soul for one's heart to be clear. One must eat it, digest it, and practice it from within on a daily basis. It is written in the Bible, "From the overflow of the heart, the mouth speaketh." (See Mathew 12:34.) For the writer, seasoned or unseasoned, it can be said that from the overflow of the heart, the hand writteth. I love this Scripture as it helps to keep us focused, becoming an important tool to measure how we're faring in our walk of faith.

Finally, I knew that my worldly manuscripts would never sell. God would not permit them to prosper because I was working against His perfect will. The desire for writing worldly issues slowly drained from my heart. I no longer would want my name associated with those writings. Their contents were not holy. Although God was in them, the story line did not revolve around Him. The legacy I choose to leave for my children, grandchildren, and future generations is that of giving honor to our Heavenly Father, Jesus, and the indwelling of the Holy Spirit. I choose to write works that will help lead others to Christ.

While enjoying the sweet comfort of sleep, I rejected the still, small voice attempting to wake me. I remember tossing from side to side trying to escape. Even in my dazed state, I recognized the voice of the Lord but, foolishly, I chose to continue my sleep. The voice of the Lord would not be ignored. God instructed me to wake up, to listen. Reluctantly, I did so. God informed me that He was preparing to pour down blessings on me so my cup would overflow. He instructed me to give-give-give, and give some more. He called to my memory the many promises I'd made that I'd bless others if my works were to sell. God was not content with my stated promise that I would do these things. He told me to get up, to write an agreement--a covenant--of the people I intended to bless with the overflow. Can you see what great and wonderful things you'd miss if you failed to listen to the voice of God? His conversation alone is worthy of waking up for; It need not be sweetened with promises. Just imagine the consequences had Moses not heeded the voice coming from the burning bush. It all breaks down to this, the best conversation of your life will always be sharing with God.

I realized that the written word would solidify it in my life. It would not be an option to change characters at a later date. A covenant is a covenant and should not be broken. It remains forever with God, it will not be broken by Him but it can be broken by people. It was nearly six o'clock on Saturday morning. Without turning on the light, I fumbled in my nightstand drawer for scratch paper and a pen and wrote six names down; five had been decided long ago. The sixth was a new person I'd recently met in the Dallas area. God already knew what my intentions were to help these people. He'd known for years and my mind had never deviated from my original intent. Therefore, it was not necessary that I write that down. He was pleased with my covenant and allowed me to return to sleep. Refreshed and happy, I naturally awoke two hours later. The memory of God's words flooded my being and I was anxious to share the memory with my daughters. I reached for the paper I'd written down the names on and went to share the good news. Having known and approved of my plans for years, they were as excited and pleased as I was.

"Though I speak
with the tongues
of men and of angels
and have not charity,
I am become
as sounding brass
or a tinkling cymbal."
1 Corinthians 13:1

"Get Up, Go To The Post Office And Get Your Money."

Chapter 34

When one does something he loves, it's impossible not to become excited about it. It's not imaginable that you can pour your heart into something and that very thing fails to flourish. There were many times I'd felt I was on the verge of a breakthrough with my writings. I'd kept a positive attitude for nine years, holding tightly to my faith that my work would sell. When my submissions were out, I'd happily make the trip to the post office in anticipation of being rewarded. Nine years is a long time to keep a positive attitude when all you're receiving is rejections. One morning God woke me up with a message.

"Get up, go to the post office and get your money," He said.

I was profoundly happy to hear this. Sitting up in bed, I stared at the clock in disappointment. It was nearly eight in the morning and the mail wouldn't be placed into the boxes until ten. I had two hours to wonder just how great my payment was and from what source it had come.

I pulled the group of envelopes from the box, flipping through them for the long awaited check. It was not there. Most assuredly, I'd overlooked it so I flipped through them again. It was not to be found. However, there was an envelope addressed to me from a self-publishing group. Immediately, I recognized this as God's guidance as to how I'd become published. This was how I'd eventually be able to go to the post office and get my money. I was neither angry nor upset, nor did I feel as though I'd been misled. I was thankful God had shown me the direction I needed to follow.

"Okay, God, if you want me to self-publish, you'll have to finance it for me," I said aloud. There was no need to explain to Him that I only worked part time as He was already aware of this.

God does not work on our timing. He moves according to His will and His will alone. We cannot rush Him with a downpour of His blessings. They're His blessings, not ours; therefore, we cannot insist that He bless us. Nor, can we force Him to give us direction. It's our job as Christians to be obedient to the Word of God. We should be ready to move when He blesses us with direction, which is a very powerful gift. His direction carries with it, life or death. David followed God's direction and was victorious in battle. If we follow His directions, the fruits of our labor will surely follow.

Whether you're writing a book or getting ready for another days work, thoughts of giving up often enter the mind. It's not easy to do but it's very easy to consider when issues have us stumped. When doing any worthwhile venture, we must keep prayed up and read up in the Word of God. Often times, those are the only truths we have to rely on. Certainly, they're the only truths we should rely on. They give us strength when we're weak and guidance when we're confused. Many a night I've tossed and turned from the pressures of the world. The Holy Word was my only comfort. Just reading it is more soothing than a day at the spa. The spa's relaxing waters have not reign to touch the soul.

Since God's gifts come in various forms, we should always be grateful for whatever gift He sends. Just as no sin is less than another, neither of God's gifts is less than another. Each is precious and should be greatly appreciated. Why should He send a second gift if we're not appreciative to the first?

NOTE: Take God's direction readily
and quickly follow it.
We delay or lose our
when not heeding His
instructions. Some
instructions only come once.

"And let us not be weary
in well doing:
for in due season
we shall reap,
if we faint not."
Galatians 6:9

Instructed To Write Memoirs

Chapter 35

Thirst for the Word of God sprang into my being and would not be quenched. Moving to the Dallas area allowed me to focus on what really mattered. I'd always known that God was the guiding force in my life. Now, separated from all the stresses of the past, I was willing to totally submit my will to Him. I began to read the Bible a few verses every night before bed, nothing in particular, just wherever the pages happened to fall when opened. Before long, the verses turned into pages and pages turned into chapters. Then I began to flip back to prior chapters for background information. It had become that interesting.

I'd never before viewed the Bible as a movie screen that cast true to life characters in living color. With no cover charge, I was awarded front row seats at whatever time I chose to view. It was remarkable. I began to tire of flipping back and decided to start from the beginning and that was a good decision. By doing so, I knew the characters, their lineages, and their contributions to the kingdom of God. My hunger for the Word continued as I read the whole Bible, Genesis through Revelation. At every opportunity, my head was buried in its pages. I was increasing my knowledge, understanding and growing spiritually at a higher rate than ever before.

I loved the growth but found myself wondering why there was such determination to finish. I'd never had an interest in reading every aspect of the Bible before, never had the desire to know more than needed for my Sunday school lesson. I knew there was a purpose in this activity so my imagination scaled the walls. Perhaps I was dying and God wanted me read up before entering heaven. Possibly at a later date, I'd lose my sight and God wanted me to read first hand before that happened. I never allowed my concern to stop my reading. Loving what

I was learning, I felt connected to the pages of the past and empowered by the knowledge.

Several months passed and I'd never questioned God for the reason, knowing He'd reveal it in time. At four minutes after one in the morning, God decided to share. He woke me up with the knowledge that I was to write a book about the visions, leading dreams, spiritual manifestations, and other times I knew I was in His presence. He did not speak the words; He dropped the knowledge into my mind and spirit. I was to correlate the times I was in His presence with passages found in the Bible. In other words, I was to line up slices of my life to documented biblical text.

At that time, I'd read the Bible with the exception of the final one hundred-fifty pages. Even as we were speaking, mentally in the spiritual realm, images were forming in my mind lining up with the Word of God. I knew what Scriptures would apply to certain situations and also knew approximately where to find them. Suddenly, I knew why it had been so important that I read the Bible as avidly as I had.

I was terribly excited and receptive to the knowledge God was imparting with me. He gave me everything I needed to write the book at that moment. He simply channeled the knowledge into my mind from the beginning to the end. I grabbed a pencil and some paper and began to write down everything He was reminding me of. Childhood memories and images from the tender age of seven suddenly became as fresh as yesterday. God allowed me to relive the moments with all my senses--seeing, hearing, smelling, feeling and tasting. He wanted me to record the details in exactness.

This time, my hand moved across the paper as though driven by turbulent yet peaceful winds. Even I was surprised by the many different occasions when I'd known I was in the presence of God. I'd never written them down before; nor had I counted them. They were ingrained within the deep well of my soul. I'd openly shared them with others at the time they'd happened and had never seen the need for documentation or chronology. In giving me this task, God blessed my heart more than one thousand fold. He allowed me to re-visit my childhood years and appreciate Mama and Daddy all the more. I was able to see their faces, hear their laughter and feel their love. It was the exact same love I was given as a child but was too young to realize its depth.

After having written the first two chapters, I sat in the den racking by brain in hopes of remembering other incidents of my childhood that I could write about. I truly enjoyed the feelings of warmth and love that emanated from Mama and Daddy and wanted to linger, to prolong this feeling as long as possible. My trying to conjure up memories proved unfruitful as nothing came to mind.

"Lois," God called from the heavens as I sat deeply in thought. "I've given you the desires of your heart. You wanted to memorialize your parents. You've done that. It's time to move on."

I immediately abated wandering and returned to the task I'd been assigned--only writing of the incidents God had refreshed my memory of. I thank Him for His wisdom and power, His holy guidance and correction.

***NOTE**:* To be used to the glory of God;
one must have an uncluttered mind.

"Let the words of my mouth,
and the meditation of my heart,
be acceptable in thy sight, 0 Lord,

my strength, and my redeemer."
Psalms 19:14

"That I may publish
with the voice of thanksgiving,
and tell of all thy wondrous works."
Psalms 26:7

Lois Snell

The Importance Of Prayer

Chapter 36

One of the most humble acts the disciples expressed was when they asked Jesus to teach them how to pray. They asked with eagerness to learn. Having walked with Jesus in a brotherhood of fellowship and servitude, they knew it was vitally important to do the will of God. Countless times they'd witnessed Jesus slipping away to a quiet corner kneeling in prayer. As Christians, we should approach the throne of God in the same manner. We should know that our communication with God should take center stage in our lives. That's what prayer is, communication with God.

The sixth chapter of Matthew gives the model prayer, the Lord's Prayer. From early childhood, the majorities of Christians have memorized this prayer and often repeat it prior to bedtime. We use it as a cure-all scapegoat. We should not only read the Scriptures, but study them as well. Had we studied these passages, we would've realized that Jesus never intended this prayer to sum up our prayer life. He told His disciples to pray "in this manner." He did not say repeat this prayer whenever you're inclined to come into the presence of the Father. Your prayers should be personal. They should mirror the complexities of your heart.

If we look back over the course of our lives, we'll find that there were countless times we were prompted with the urge to pray. The urge was real whether we responded to it or not. It was a request from God to come into His presence. He desired to talk to us.

Prayer acknowledges God as your One and True personal Savior. It lifts praises to the King of Glory. Prayer is the key that will unlock the floodgates of Heaven to numerous blessings. It's an act of freewill that will sail you through troubled waters without thought of drowning. It is essential to healthy and wholesome living.

You will never feel the ache of loneliness when you're knelt down in prayer. You are not alone. God's presence can heal a wounded heart; it can heal a crippling soul. The fear of the unknown vanishes in His presence: Problems diminish and pains become dull or completely disappear. All other issues pale in comparison when our minds and hearts are focused on the Most High God.

I've always kept an ongoing prayer life. It never mattered where I was, driving down the street or sitting quietly in the pew. I knew that God heard a frantic "Help!" as well as long drawn out wailings from within. He keeps His angels encamped around those that believe in Him to aid them in times of trouble.

Although God hears and responds to frantic cries, don't allow those to become the substance of your prayer life. God wants you to commune with Him even when danger is not visible. He wants to be the lifeline to your soul not merely the embodiment of your person. He wants to know that you're well-grounded in His Word and lean on Him for your next breath. By leaning on Him and being grounded in His Word, you're conditioning your heart to do His will. You'll be better equipped to handle the pressures of the world and respond in a godly fashion by maintaining a healthy prayer life.

There were times that I was extremely tired when prompted to pray. Sometimes I'd already gone to bed and had prayed before I'd retired. Comfortable, I was reluctant to climb out of bed and fall to my knees. Many times, I didn't. I simply prayed from where I was or ignored the urge entirely. This is wrong. It is never okay to ignore the voice of God. Whether the voice resonates in your ear, tugs at your heart or is ingrained within your mind, it is not to be ignored or brushed aside. God said in His Word, harden not your heart the day you hear my voice. Whenever we do, we miss the blessings associated with the Blessed. Who are we to ignore our Creator? Who are we to discriminately choose when and when not to speak to God? This is a very dangerous way to live because we never know if this is our last opportunity to pray. We never know what wonderful benefits or revelations will be derived from our prayer.

Why do we need to kneel? Good question. This act shows humility. It shows that you honor the Holy One and are willing to conform to His will. It offers silent praises within itself. I once asked my prayer instructor, Pastor Rick Jordan of Concord, if it were necessary to always kneel in prayer. After all, there are those who are physically impaired. Pastor Jordan explained that God listens to the position of one's heart. God examines the heart and knows what's there. Therefore, the position of the heart, whether sincere, evasive, dutiful or scornful, is recognized by God and that position determines your reverence to Him.

In prayer, we should first acknowledge God. We should openly give Him praises and honor, as He alone is worthy of them. Jesus did it, as He walked the earth, even the essence of His being was rooted in prayer. Jesus said, "Our Father, which art in heaven, hallowed be Thy name." Jesus identified to whom He was speaking, calling Him by name, Our Father. To eliminate confusion with carnal living, He added "which art in heaven." Therefore, it's not your earthly father. "Hallowed be thy name" means forever lit up, crowned in glory for everyone to see. Spend some time there, glorifying and praising God. We should then confess every known sin and ask forgiveness of them and those committed unknowingly. Next, we should come to God in thanksgiving for the countless blessings He's bestowed on us. At that point, we should make our supplications known. That is, whatever our special requests are, we should ask God in all humility knowing that He hears and cares for us. Be alert in prayer, focused on the true and living God. Remember the words of Jesus, "And whatsoever ye shall ask in my name, that will I do, that the Father will be glorified in the Son," John 14:13. Keep in mind that asking in Jesus' name with an insincere heart and for things ungodly avails nothing. Neither Jesus nor God will bless such actions.

It's not always necessary to talk when we pray. Communication with God is always a two-way conversation. Sometimes the act of falling to your knees and opening your heart is all that's needed. If we're extremely troubled, the Holy Spirit will intervene for us. The Apostle Paul wrote that the Holy Spirit conveys groaning that cannot be uttered. (Romans 8:26) If we submit to God in quiet humbleness, we put ourselves in perfect position to hear from Him. I know for a fact that He will converse with us, that is, if we're open and willing to listen. Sometimes your prayer should be quiet respect, lifting holy hands and a heart filled with praise to an awesome and just God.

The key to a good prayer life is sincerity. I can't stress this enough. You must be honest and sincere with God to insure His willingness to acknowledge you. You can't stay in His grace by pumping your prayer life with lies. Good intentions are lies if they're not carried out. You can't sway God with good intentions because He knows the intricate workings of your heart. He created you. He cannot be deceived. He already knows whether or not your promises are empty utterances.

It's a good thing, a right thing, to pray. Like Jesus, David—a man after God's own heart—was forever deep in prayer. His prayers guided him successfully through many blood shod wars and left David physically unscarred. Many have questioned how David could be a man after God's own heart since he was a peeping tom, and later caused the unwarranted death of Bathsheba's husband. David, no less human than you and I, was subject to all the desires of the flesh. He was a king; death sentences were carried out at his command, he was a man to be feared. Thereby, he was granted privileges not available to most. David was a man after God's own heart before he'd sinned. After he'd committed the sins of indulgence in an illicit affair with Bathsheba and causing the death of her husband, David took his sins to God. Through prayer and supplication, he petitioned the forgiveness of God. He was earnest and sincere in his prayers. He tried as best he could to right the wrongs he'd done. God felt the pain of his heart and forgave him. His sincerity caused him to continue to be a man after God's own heart.

You'll find chapter after chapter of biblical readings where insurmountable obstacles were overcome through prayer. The story is always the same. People stray as far as they can from God. They find themselves ensnared in all the evils of the world, often bought on by their own hands. They want swift relief from their ailments. After trying practically everything else, they turn back to God. God has been faithful and just to forgive His people; but, He only forgives when the heart is sincere. For the most part, we know when we're committing sin. We should keep in mind that there may not be time to get things right with God. Death often catches people unprepared and quite by surprise. The Word says to lean not to your own understanding. Your understanding is different than God's.

In each of us, God has placed the ability to succeed. He has placed a talent, a gift that is unique to us. Many of us have multiple gifts, none greater than the other, just different. Oftentimes, we don't recognize our gifts and stumble through the wilderness of life seeking our rightful place. We search for many years without obtaining the desired results. We seek guidance in friends, in counselors, in clergy and sometimes in strangers. When all that is needed is that we seek it in prayer. Living biblically is as simple as applying the words of the bible to your everyday life. It will quickly become a habit if you exert a little effort in the beginning.

Answers to your problems can be found in prayer. That's why we should pray without ceasing. The life and crucifixion of Jesus Christ is the perfect example. Throughout Jesus' walk on earth, He was constantly in prayer, constantly communing with the Father. Even in His greatest pain, torn and bleeding flesh, hanging among robbers and thieves on a wooden cross at Calvary, He was in communication with God. Rather than asking Him to repair His hands and blast the Roman Soldiers with fire, He requested: "Father, forgive them; for they know not what they do." Luke 23:34. We can make it through any hardship if we are in continuous communication with God. Any hardship. We all know there is a higher being, we cry out to Him in times of need. We all seek answers that are beyond our understanding. Often times, God will drop the knowledge into our spirits. Other times, when we're preparing to deal with the problem, we'll find that it has dissipated. It's true that when praises go up, blessings come down.

Another thing that's of utmost importance is when God says "no", He means ***"NO!"*** If He's given you a solid no, let it be. Don't bicker with Him about it. Don't attempt to argue your point or use your earthly reasoning with Him. You cannot change God's mind with tears. He knows what's best for you and your future, my future, was written before either of us was born. This is when your faith must carry you to places you cannot see. Have faith in God's decision because He alone is worthy of making it. You only have the knowledge of the present and vague remembrances of the past. Even your present is limited to mortal lines of vision. God sees far beyond that, He sees your first and last breaths. He sees your entire lineage, before and after your life span. Trust Him, trust His plan as it's far better than yours. I've heard it said to never put a question mark where God's placed a period. This message carries a wealth of blessings for those who willingly adhere to it. It's alright to argue your point with humans as they may not have your best interest at heart. But, God designed humanity. If you're having trouble accepting the "no" He's placed in your life, pray for guidance in accepting it. Why burden yourself trying to chart a path through the wilderness when God has already made the crooked places straight?

You may wonder for whom you should pray. I've found it beneficial to pray for everyone. Don't limit yourself to those you love. Some of us may not have enough to keep us employed in prayer should we do this. Invariably, there are people who have decided, through no fault of your own, to become your enemy. Perhaps they don't like the way you wear your hair or the color of your eyes. Possibly you remind them of someone they knew before, someone they either loved or hated. Most often, it's because your principles vastly differ than theirs and they've not embraced the logic that others are just as entitled. Should there be people that for some reason you don't like, you need to pray for them and your oppressors in particular. God requires that we love all people. Most often, that comes easier than liking them because we know God lives in each of us and we can choose to love the God living inside those we don't like. If they've caused you harm, unwarranted stress, lied on you or mocked you—pray for them. They need not know of your prayers as it may become a greater source of agitation to them. It should be private, between you and Jesus. They're hurting, perhaps unknown to themselves, and may only feel release from their pain by causing pain to others. Try as best you can to look beyond the pain, to focus on the distant future. Don't try to rectify the situation by acting out in anger. "Vengeance is mine; I will repay, saith the Lord." (Romans 12:19) Don't attempt to do God's job for Him.

You don't need to be present when God repays your oppressor.

Our carnal natures nearly always dictate that we should find pleasure in the repayment of oppressors. God would have no man gloat in another's distress. God will repay as He promised, so think on the good things of life. Rely on God to fight your battle for you. Don't weaken your spirit with the weaknesses of others. You must always rise above pettiness and revenge. God wants our hearts free to act in His image. Sometimes, your actions are the only images others will see God through.

For whom should you pray? Yourself, your loved ones, of course you should. In fact, you're so good at it; you don't need instruction, but, do venture out. Become an intercessor on behalf of others. Practice praying for strangers you meet, accident victims on the road, a child displaced from a parent in the mall. Pray for people you see waiting for the bus during a rainstorm or homeless people underneath the highways. Pray for both strangers and acquaintances with distress filled eyes. You need not know what the problem is, God does. There's always someone needing our help in prayer and Jesus is ever ready for us to shine His light on earth.

Prayer changes things. Prayer is essential to physical and mental health. It is your right and your duty to take your cares to God, to commune with Him from the holy temple that is your body. In everyone's heart, God has placed the need to pray. Don't deny yourself the cleansing it allows you. Don't deny God the joy of forgiving you and teaching you the good and perfect way. Prayer does change things. It changes our hearts and our lives. It lifts burdens of the heavy-laden.

It causes the fool to become wise. It reassures the soul of those blessed with wisdom. It chases fear from our hearts. More important than all, it acknowledges God as Savior and lifts praises to Him. There is no substitute for prayer.

"But thou, when thou prayest,
enter into thy closet,
and when thou hast shut thy door,
pray to thy Father
which is in secret; and thy Father
which seeth in secret
shall reward thee
openly"
Matthew 6:6

"And he spake
a parable unto them
to this end, that men
ought always to pray,
and not to faint."
Luke 18:1

Lois Snell

Tithing, Re-visited

Chapter 37

Neither God nor Jesus Himself dealt with me one-on-one about the issue of tithing. That is, not in a sense that I can directly relate. However, I do remember my friend sharing her testimony of tithing. She and her husband had recently moved back to her hometown and salaries there were not as lucrative as they'd been in Oklahoma City. Yet, they'd decided to tithe. In less than three weeks, their financial picture began to change for the better. She was convinced the change came only after their deep commitment to tithing. I've come to believe that was God whispering to me through her vocal chords. Nothing is by chance; every conversation has meaning even if it's simply to learn from other's experiences.

I'd been in church all my life and not one sermon had convicted me to the point of becoming a thither. It is quite possible that the sermon had been preached, perhaps many times. Yet, in my carnal state, I neither heard it nor received it. This is one of the many reasons why we're instructed to read the Bible for ourselves. If you don't hear it, through preaching of the Word or reading on your own, you're not likely to become convicted to move in the direction God would have you go. The source of your wealth comes from God. The source of your wealth is God. His manual dictates how we should handle it.

During the years I'd struggled financially while raising my children, I was constantly giving away their clothing. These items were still in fine condition, some they'd not yet outgrown or ever worn. Working in retail, I was able to cash in on the reductions as they hit the floor. Also, I found lovely items at garage sales for pennies on the dollar. My sister, Charlene, always purchased more than one outfit for my daughters on their birthdays and at Christmas. Another sister, Maxine, living in Tacoma, Washington, sent checks at Christmas time.

My sister, Ivy, continued to send boxes of clothing and accessories. As much and as often as I gave, our closets were always filled with lovely clothing. I didn't realize it at the time, but I was tithing in apparel and God was granting one hundred percent increase.

Though He continued to make provisions for us, I've come to learn that my financial struggles lasted longer than was necessary due to the fact that I ignored God's basic rule of tithing. My sisters and cousins had purchased lovely homes; yet, I continued renting lovely homes or townhouses. Occasionally, I noticed co-workers and friends who shared the same economic status as myself; yet, they'd purchased while I'd rented. I admired them for their money handling skills while admonishing myself for my lack thereof. They'd tithed while I'd made excuses. Never connecting these facts, I'd observed God rewarding their efforts yet still extending the hand of mercy to those, like myself, continuing to walk in disobedience. God is faithful even when we're not.

Neighborhood children were always welcome at my table. I've witnessed adults sending their children's playmates home when dinner was ready. This is cruel and insensitive because these children have sometimes helped to influence the menu and the aromas have teased their taste buds. I willingly gave food to charitable organizations or to those I knew who were in need. Sometimes I went shopping for the parties and sometimes I shopped from the bounty of my cabinets and freezer. Never were my cupboards barren. I didn't realize it at the time, but I was tithing in foodstuffs, and God was granting one hundred percent increase.

Openly sharing my belief in God and Jesus, I've been blessed by testimonies of work associates, friends, relatives and strangers. I've been blessed by stories of strength when mine was waning. I've been rewarded by not hearing the dirty jokes flagrantly told to and enjoyed by others. I've been rewarded by not having profanity spoken in my presence. I was tithing in witnessing, and God has granted one hundred percent increase.

We must be cognizant of what we're tithing and what to expect from it. Previously, I didn't realize I was tithing anything and felt I was simply being blessed. God was blessing me—through His grace—and because I was tithing. Yet, I'd never gotten around to the issue of tithing money. I've heard people say and have used these statements myself, "I may not give my ten percent, but I give my time. God understands." This is a poor excuse for a child of God. And yes, God does understand. He understands you're not tithing ten percent of the money He allows you to earn. A person who gives his time earns a vacation. That is a reasonable expectation for tithing time.

In His Word, God tells us to tithe money. The first fruit nowadays represents money—cash. Why? The mortgage payment of the church cannot be paid by the time I tithe to it. The witness I share with others won't pay the electric bills because faith without works is dead, God said. Foodstuffs are wonderful for hungry people but the church is hungry for the Living Word. The Living Word is to be administered by just prophets of God and the Bible states they are to be compensated for their impartation. Since we no longer operate on the barter system, prophets need cash to meet their obligations. Clothing donated to a worthy cause is commendable, but God's Word says to give no thought to what you'll wear tomorrow. God would have you clothed in wisdom and reverence to His Holy Word. Then, He will dress you as splendidly as He's dressed the lilies of the field.

Do you remember how Jesus was moved with compassion when the widow woman put in her last two cents? Can you even imagine how

He must have blessed her? No, it's not stated in the Bible that He did but His very nature of healing, giving, and saving souls dictates that He did. This woman gave money—cash, not silks, satins, oils or fish. Do not deceive yourself by thinking you're doing God's will by tithing with extra clothing, foodstuffs and free time He's blessed you with. You're robbing God by doing so. You're robbing Him of the money His servants need to effectively operate His body, the church. You're robbing Him of His desire to throw open the gates of heaven and pour down blessings too many for you to receive. Keep in mind that you have no bargaining power with God. He set the rules thousands of years before you were born. If you allow these good works (and they are good works) to become the substance of your tithe, you'll be willing participants in Satan's deception.

God only requires ten percent of our earnings. It's affordable. Look and listen, the only people that complain about tithing are those that don't. They haven't come into the realization that God can do more with their ten percent than they can do with the ninety.

Lastly, everything you've become, everything you've earned belongs to God. That is, the whole of your check, the whole of your certificates of deposit, stocks and bonds, the whole of your earnings or holdings. Every entry listed on your asset sheet belongs to God. He created the circumstances to make it possible for you to obtain these things. Since God loves a cheerful giver, I strongly encourage you to give your ten percent plus a generous offering. It's not too much to ask. It's only your reasonable service. We must realize deep down in our hearts that it's not an option to tithe or not to tithe. It's a commandment.

NOTE:
Good works can never
Purchase
Tickets to Heaven.

"But this I say,
He which soweth sparingly
shall reap also sparingly;
and he that soweth bountifully
shall reap also bountifully.
Every man according as
he purposeth in his heart,
so let him give; not grudgingly,
or of necessity;
for God loveth
a cheerful giver."
II Corinthians 9:6-7

After Thoughts And Summation

Chapter 38

This book was written so others may realize when they're in the presence of God. Many excuse His miracles, His presence, and His mercy as trickery of sorts. God is all around us; you can neither escape nor ignore Him. There are serious consequences levied on those of us who try. If you need proof of this, ask Jonah. How would you question a man who's been dead for many centuries? Read his book in the Bible. It will answer every question you ask. Jonah felt he could escape God by taking a ship traveling the opposite direction than where God ordered him to go. He was allowed three days in the belly of a giant whale to reflect on his decision. We are to learn from biblical truths and avoid as many pitfalls as possible.

There are many rolls of film of my life that I would've chosen to leave unexposed. Once repented and forgiven, we like to bury our sins and remember them no more. Therefore, this book is not written as an expose of myself: I know its contents, I've lived it. Under commission of God, it was written so others may benefit from like situations. It was written so others may realize that God loves them regardless of their past. It was written so you'll have another first-hand accounting that God will forgive you of every sin. You cannot escape His love, but you can escape His grace. Be mindful of His laws but be more mindful of His Son, Jesus, who walked among men—praying, preaching, healing and saving souls. His Son is the Word that became flesh that men might see, that men might touch, that men might believe. Jesus paid it all, giving His life as a ransom for many—all that would believe. He had the power to lay His life down, and by His power, He raised it up again. Jesus suffered for you and me. He paid the ultimate price for our salvation. All we need to do is believe it in our hearts (Jesus Christ has come in the flesh, died for our sins and was raised on the third day, He lives!) and profess it with our mouths. Jesus is the Door, the only Door that leads to the Father, the only Door that leads to salvation. Believe in Him.

I realize that biblical Scriptures are written in a sequence of events and mainly pertain to the sequence in which they were written. However, many Scriptures speak to your heart becoming rhema words spoken to your specific situation. The Scriptural references at the end of each chapter are such. They are not mutations of the Holy Bible. They are rhema words spoken to my soul. God commissioned the Bible to be written to be of great benefit to His people. It keeps one grounded as to whom God is and gives the reader a glimpse of His infinite power. Also, the Bible becomes a road map to weary travelers, lost in their walk of faith.

Many find it difficult to relate the Bible to their present day lifestyles. Before you read, you should first pray for understanding. You should then read the Bible for yourself. Allow your imagination to convert chariots into cars, swords into guns and ships into airplanes. You'll find the heart of man is the same now as it was then. We are still a rebellious people, stubbornly ignoring the rules of God and making a mockery of His laws. Men still seek the delight of many women instead of committing wholly to his chosen one. Treasure seekers and spoilers (thieves) have never ceased. Back-biters, liars, they are as rampant now as then. Murderers and rapists are still seeking their next victim. Inventors of good and terrible devices are still burning the midnight oil. Gay issues didn't come out of the closet thirty years ago; they boldly danced down the streets of Sodom and Gommerah. History is constantly repeating itself. Get connected with God and know your source. Trust in the revelations He'll allow you to glimpse when studying His Word. If you've not cultivated that deep level of trust, there's an unlimited supply of concordances, bible reference books and commentaries available for your help. For the most part, these books are written by master theologians and highly praised by others. They're widely distributed and used in seminary colleges and universities. Excellent points of reference; they're a staple for teaching ministers the deeper meaning of God's Word. Utilizing them, it better equips the lay person the mysteries of God. God's love provides for you even before you seek knowledge from His manual on life.

Mere humans, we want to give credence to God's Holy name the way we choose to do it. We don't ask His permission. We chart our own course and expect Him to bless it because, "We're doing it in His name." When the fact is, it's our agenda, not His. A good idea is not always a godly idea and every good idea should not become your mission in life. It's important to know where your calling lies and work within that parameter.

Whether we choose to believe it or not, God has raised up many a person to write the book we have burning in our hearts to write, or to sing the song we love to sing. He's raised up many a shut womb to mother the children we've given birth to. We need Him. He does not need us.

Are you aware that success can be achieved while praising God your way? You can become so successful you'll never realize you're outside the will of God. Seek God's favor in all you do and only work in the areas that are pleasing to Him. Don't allow Satan to build a stronghold in your life. By then, he'll have greater success in winning your soul to hell as well as those you've influenced. Where is the gratification in that? Regardless to appearances, you're on the battlefield every day. You must read the Word of God to be able to fight against forces seen and unseen. The accuser does not play fair. He will use the tender mercies of your own heart against you. His ultimate goals are always the same—to hand deliver invitations to hell.

A word from God is all that's needed to save you. If you don't know Him, you won't know how to ask for His help. If you don't read His Word to become closer to Him, you may never be able to decipher when you're in His presence. God wants a relationship with you. You were granted life for that purpose. He loves you more than mortal words can express, more than you can ever imagine. God wants to quicken the good spirits that lie dormant within your soul. He wants you to experience His cleansing, His joy. Never think you're so far removed from God that He will never hear your prayer. You must be earnest in your prayer life, true and open with God. He knows your innermost thoughts anyway so it's impossible to deceive Him. There will always be consequences to deal with for our actions and our peers judge us more harshly than God does. Certainly, they're less forgiving. If you're sinning now, or have sinned yesterday or eighty-five years ago, and you're genuinely remorseful for these actions, God is willing to forgive you. Ask Him in all sincerity and know that He hears.

There are many ways of knowing when you're in the presence of God. This book has chronicled many instances when I knew. Now that you've seen through my eyes, it's my greatest hope that you'll use this knowledge. Use it to open your eyes and ears to God's tender tapping on your heart. Looking back over the course of your life, you'll realize that He's been there all along.

When knowledge, clear as a bell, drops in your spirit and it lines up with the Word of God, you're in His presence. When dreams of clarity carry you away to near or distant places while giving you needed guidance, you're in His presence. When the voice of reason speaks in a still small voice and it lines up with the Word of God, you're in His presence. When the voice of righteousness resonates within your soul, you're in His presence. When a peaceful calm comes over you during the most turbulent of storms, you're in His presence. In the midst of a quiet moment, when all is well with you, you're in His presence. When you're reading His Word, and clarity of meaning surrounds you, you're in His presence. God is ever present with us; He said so in his Word. His Word is the only truth you can solely rely on. He is that invisible force that keeps us from destruction. He is the Provider of the very air that we breathe. Whether you see evidence of the Most High God or not, you're in His presence.

"And Jesus came
and spake unto them, saying,
All power is given unto me
in heaven and in earth
Go ye therefore,
and teach all nations,
baptizing them in the name
of the Father, and of the Son,
and of the Holy Ghost:
Teaching them to observe
all things whatsoever
I have commanded you:
and, lo,
I am with you always,
even until the
end of the world.
Amen."
Matthew 28: 18-20

Scriptural references that line up with my life

IN HIS PRESENCE…Witnessing The Glory of God

My Testimony…Times I Knew I Was IN HIS PRESENCE .

IN HIS PRESENCE…Witnessing The Glory of God

My Testimony…Times I Knew I Was IN HIS PRESENCE

Look for other works by Lois Snell

Renaissance of The Soul

Lineage

Through The Valley

www.loissnell.com

About The Cover Artist

Marvin Huckaby earned his BA from the University of Texas at Dallas. Working in a variety of mediums, he creates thought provoking scenes ranging from land, air and seascapes to still life and personal portraits. A perfectionist in his craft, Marvin has the unique ability to create visual masterpieces from prose. His target market also includes book cover designs and book illustrations.

"Abstract representation of ideas, social commentary and symbolism are the tools I use to answer the question, what do I, as an artist, have to say." Marvin Huckaby

Mr. Marvin Huckaby
mhuckaby75@hotmail.com

www.ingramcontent.com/pod-product-compliance
Lightning Source LLC
LaVergne TN
LVHW051625080426
835511LV00016B/2181
* 9 7 8 0 9 7 0 7 8 4 6 0 5 *